KNOW MORE ABOUT YOURSELF AND YOUR LOVER

Here at last is a book that fully explores male sexuality. Ranging from an explanation of the "koro syndrome" to a detailed inquiry into the effects of cocaine during sex, MALE SEXUAL FUNCTION offers a candid, contemporary look at a wide variety of topics:

- Psychological and physical causes of impotence

- Fallacies about heart attacks, masturbation, VD, and vasectomy in relation to male sexuality

- What not to do during a period of impotency

- Other sexual crises (including declining orgasmic intensity)

DR. RICHARD MILSTEN received his B.A. from Yale University and his M.D. from Columbia University, The College of Physicians and Surgeons. A board certified urologist, he is a member of the American Urologic Association, the American Medical Association, and a Fellow of the American College of Surgeons. Dr. Milsten is currently serving as an attending physician to several New Jersey hospitals, as well as maintaining a private practice.

MALE SEXUAL FUNCTION

Myth, Fantasy & Reality

Dr. Richard Milsten

AVON
PUBLISHERS OF BARD, CAMELOT AND DISCUS BOOKS

MALE SEXUAL FUNCTION MYTH, FANTASY, REALITY
is an original publication of Avon Books.
This work has never before appeared in book form.

AVON BOOKS
A division of
The Hearst Corporation
959 Eighth Avenue
New York, New York 10019

First Avon Printing, May, 1979

Printed in the U.S.A.

To my mother and father, who provided me with the education to become a physician; and to my wife, who encouraged and assisted me along the way.

CONTENTS

I love such books as are either easy and entertaining, and that tickle my fancy, or such as give me comfort and offer counsel in reordering my life.

—Montaigne

Contents

Contents

Contents

ACKNOWLEDGMENTS

As a practicing urologist, my spare time was limited. By necessity I wrote only in the evenings and on weekends, and many people adjusted their schedules to assist me. This book would not have been completed without their enthusiastic help, which I gratefully acknowledge here.

Helen Metcalfe, who assisted me in library research and procured hundreds of scientific articles, constantly called my attention to relevant material.

Cynthia Norton, a master typist and organizer, prepared all of the drafts leading to the final manuscript. Her scrupulous attention to detail made my work much easier.

Louise Geary proofread with a keen eye toward spelling and grammar.

Barbara Morgan and Joe Hotchkiss provided invaluable advice; their editorial expertise is demonstrated on every page of this book.

Alan Wein, M.D., an active researcher in the treatment of impotence, offered advice to ensure scientific accuracy.

Many friends read the manuscript and made helpful suggestions regarding content and style.

My wife, Nancy, read and reread, arranged and rearranged this book, and encouraged me all the way.

I gratefully acknowledge all of their help.

—R.M.

FOREWORD

Frequently, a man who is impotent will seek help from a urologist. This is one of the most frustrating problems the urologist faces. Because many of these cases are psychological in origin, the treatment often consists of a long period of discussion with the use of medication kept at a minimum.

The troubled patient is often hesitant in discussing his sexual problems with his physician. The following pattern often unfolds: the patient complains of prostate trouble or bladder symptoms; an examination is completed and the findings fail to disclose any signs of illness or disease; the patient, as he is about to leave, adds as an afterthought, "Doctor, I'm also having trouble with my sex life." In reality, this is why he sought advice in the first place but was hesitant and embarrassed to talk about it.

This book, *Male Sexual Function: Myth, Fantasy and Reality,* is most timely. It covers the subject of impotence and deals with other male sexual problems in a clear, easily understood manner. It offers solace and solutions to the many men and women who are bewildered by these disorders and seek help. By understanding normal sexual function and the various problems which may develop, a sexual crisis may be prevented.

Foreword

A few years ago, while serving as President of the American Medical Association, I found it necessary to hold office hours—almost on an emergency basis—on my short visits home. Once, an old friend came to see me. He was complaining of sex problems and after a long discussion on the various causes of impotency, I commented, "Ralph, I can understand your feelings. You and I are about the same age and I have the same trouble."

He replied without hesitation: "I need help, not sympathy."

Charles A. Hoffman, M.D.
Past President
American Medical Association

Man can endure earthquake, epidemic, dreadful disease, every form of spiritual torment; but the most dreadful tragedy that can befall him is and will remain the tragedy of the bedroom.

—Tolstoy

CHAPTER I
WHY THIS BOOK WAS WRITTEN

I am still learning.
—Michelangelo

All normal males, at some time in their lives, will find themselves unable to have an erection. This problem is not confined to the middle-aged and the elderly, but also happens to teenagers and males in their twenties and thirties. For some men this condition develops suddenly and is transient, while for others it may come on gradually and persist as a chronic problem. Men whose sexual performance has been successful for years may one day find themselves unable to achieve an erection. This has been experienced even by males who have regarded themselves as marathon bedroom performers.

Difficulty in maintaining or inability to have an erection is only one of the sexual crises that men may experience. Others are:

1. Uncontrollable ejaculation: Men complain that ejaculation occurs too quickly to allow sexual satisfaction either for themselves or for their female partner.
2. Inability to ejaculate: Despite a normal erection, the sexual act may go on for as long as an hour, but no ejaculation occurs.
3. Decreased quality of orgasm: Some males complain that while they can have an erection and ejaculate, the orgasm is not as intense as it once was.

17

4. Loss of interest in sex: Many men are distressed because sexual activity is no longer exciting.

The effect of these potentially devastating events on the male and the female partner is variable, but those who are knowledgeable about these problems will be better able to cope with them. The information in this book is intended not only for those males and their female partners who are currently having difficulty with sexual functioning, but also for those who are presently enjoying a seemingly normal sexual life. All males should be aware of the sexual problems they may encounter, and females should acquaint themselves with the causes of these problems so that they can either help to avert them or assist their male partner when a difficulty does occur.

Implications of Inadequate Sexual Performance

It is almost impossible for the female to realize the degree of fear that the male has when his sexual performance is inadequate. If a female doesn't have an orgasm during every sexual encounter, she probably isn't alarmed. She generally attributes her inability to achieve orgasm to the fact that she just wasn't in the mood. But if a male doesn't have an erection, he generally regards it as a disaster. For impotence means more than simply not being able to achieve an erection. It represents the destruction of a man's self-image. His self-confidence and self-respect dwindle. And if he cannot achieve an erection on repeated occasions and thus fails his female partner, she may become sexually unresponsive. The male then begins to complain that his partner is frigid and not interested in sexual activity. Hence a vicious cycle is created.

A male's inadequate sexual performance affects many areas of his life. On the job he may be less effective because of his preoccupation with his sexual inadequacy. At home he may be depressed and short-tempered. His wife or female partner may become increasingly dissatisfied, and the possibility that the relationship will break up becomes more and more real. It is a fact that the divorce rate in this country is soaring, and one of the reasons most often cited is lack of sexual satisfaction at home.

It is unfortunate but true that the quality of the sexual lives of most men and women is not as satisfactory as it should be. Interviews with couples who are apparently happily married, financially secure, and who have never openly spoken of divorce reveal that from a sexual standpoint many are lonely, disappointed, frustrated, and emotionally dissatisfied.

A survey of psychiatrists on sources of sexual conflict in marriage [1] is very revealing. Based on their clinical experience with patients, the psychiatrists made the following observations: most men believe that their marital sexual relations are too infrequent. Most women desire longer foreplay and believe that coitus itself is too brief. Most men desire their wives to participate more actively in sexual relations, and many wives are displeased with their husbands' sexual manner or technique. Most women also desire more postcoital affection than they presently receive. Finally, most couples have conflicting attitudes about engaging in oral-genital sex.

It is apparent that many couples find their sexual relationships less than ideal. This rocky foundation provides a natural setting for the development of sexual dysfunction.

In men love-inadequacy is increasing to an alarming degree, and impotence has come to be a disorder associated with modern civilization. Every impotent man forms the nucleus of a love tragedy, for impotence makes marriage impossible or may be the cause of an ill-fated one. It also undermines the health of the women, and has an equally pernicious effect on the mental lives of both husbands and wives. [2]

This statement aptly describing the damaging effect of

19

male sexual problems on modern society was written more than fifty years ago by a physician named Wilhelm Stekel.

Conversations I have had with patients in my office provide a great deal of insight into how sexual difficulties affect their everyday lives. During these discussions, long-imprisoned and bothersome thoughts are suddenly released. It is easy to discern the mental and emotional relief that a male gains by being able to reveal a problem that has too long been contained. The following comments are indicative of the depth of discomfort that many men experience. They were made in response to questions I asked during interviews with some of my male patients who had come for sexual counseling.

1. *Do you think about your sexual problem often?*

It is with me all the time. I cannot shake it. When getting ready for bed it bothers me the most. I would like to try sex but I know there is no use.

How can you forget about it? Everything you see in the movies or on television has something to do with sex. Every novel I seem to read describes sexual encounters. You go to a party and all the guys are talking about sexual conquests or telling jokes with sexual connotations.

The problem is always on my mind except while I am concentrating at work. And even that has become more difficult. There are many young secretaries with tight skirts and loose blouses and when I see them I think about how nice it would be to be able to have intercourse. I am single and I guess I am lucky that I don't have a woman who I have to satisfy, though I would like to if I could.

I don't think there is a day that goes by that I don't wish that I was able to have an erection. My wife and I don't talk about it and I have never discussed it with my friends, but it is on my mind. I haven't had intercourse for two years and I felt by now I would be used to it and it wouldn't bother me. But it does.

2. *Has your sexual problem affected your own self-image?*

Very definitely! I am forty-two years old and never felt this would happen to me. I don't feel like a complete man. When you can't satisfy your wife, how can you satisfy yourself?

I always wondered what it would be like to be without a penis. Now I know. It's there but it only hangs and doesn't seem to be useful for any purpose except going to the bathroom. Every time I void I take it into my hand and am reminded that I am not normal.

I've lost confidence. My wife says it doesn't matter, but I don't think she respects me as much any more. There is no reason my teenage children should know about the problem, but I really wonder if they do? I'm sure my wife hasn't told them, but somehow I think they must know.

You know that old saying about who wears the pants in the family. I still make the major decisions but wonder if I really have the right to do so. After all I don't meet all my responsibilities as a man at home.

3. *Does your wife or female partner understand the problem?*

She knows there is something wrong but isn't certain what. We still try to have relations but it doesn't seem to work. Sometimes she seems satisfied but I don't know why she would be.

My wife fully understands my difficulty. We even

had sexual counseling. At first she thought I had another woman, but fortunately this idea has been cleared up. Things are better than they were. I now satisfy her with masturbation.

My wife doesn't understand and doesn't care. One night she told me not to start something I couldn't finish and I haven't tried since. . . . I've thought about trying sex with another woman, but I don't think I would be any more successful.

4. *Has your inability to function successfuly sexually affected your daily life?*

I'm depressed. At first I only seemed to be troubled at night. It seemed that I would lie awake for hours thinking about what I couldn't do. Now, I cannot concentrate on my work. I seem to spend more time trying to do things.

I work on an assembly line and I've got plenty of time for free thought. My job is mechanical and very boring. No day passes that I don't think about my problem in one way or another. It is taking me longer to do things than before.

Nothing is like it used to be. I don't sleep as well, eat as well, or work as well.

5. *Have you ever sought advice or thought about seeking advice from a friend?*

Are you kidding? I wouldn't let anyone know about this.

The closest I got was once telling a joke about an impotent man. I thought that might open a discussion, but my friend only laughed and said, "I'm sure glad I don't have that problem." I wished I had never told the joke.

It's funny that you mention it. My closest friend and I discuss financial matters all the time and we even know each other's salary. But I would never tell him I couldn't get an erection.

My friend told me he was having a problem with sex. I never would have brought it up first. We had a long talk and both decided we were just getting older.

6. *What would it mean to you to be able to function normally again?*

A whole new life.

It would make me very happy and I know my wife would be pleased.

I suppose it would mean a great deal, but I've just about given up hope.

They say the greatest things in life are free. But now I find that even trying to have sex again is going to cost me money.

What good am I this way?

I would like to say I could take it or leave it. But truthfully, I'd be a lot happier man if I were normal again.

The Education Gap

Unfortunately, our society assumes that men are automatically experienced in the art of sex. The male is often expected to take the lead in any sexual encounter. The most traumatic example of this is on the wedding night. While the number of men and women who remain virginal until marriage is decreasing, many couples come to their wedding night with little or no sexual experience. And in these instances almost everything is left up to the male. His new wife expects him to know what to do, while in truth he may not only be uncertain whether he is going to be able to have an erection, but when he does, he may not know where the erect penis is supposed to be placed. The extreme example of this lack of knowledge is found in marriages that have never been consummated. A certain percentage of couples who seek help for sexual difficulties relate that they have never had intercourse. One interesting study [3] involved 1,000 white American females with an average age of twenty-nine years. None of these women had consummated a relationship with their husband, yet had been married an average of eight years. Many reasons were cited: fear of pain during penetration, the belief that sex is evil, dislike of the penis, concern about pregnancy, fear of injuring the male's penis, and lack of knowledge about how to have intercourse. An impotent husband ranked high on the list. While it may be difficult to believe, some couples have lived together for as long as twenty years without ever successfully completing the sex act.

In this country, where the standard of living and education ranks among the highest in the world, we are grossly ignorant about many areas of sexual functioning. Despite recent advances in understanding the physiology of the human sexual response, the average male and female know very little about the cause and effect of a male's inadequate sexual performance. We pride ourselves on caring for our newborn and on educating our children both at school and at home. We instruct them on what to eat and what clothes to wear; and we assist them in getting along with their peers. As children become teenagers, we assign them more and more responsibility in order to ensure their smooth transition into adulthood. We provide them with instruction on how to drive a car and how to become competent in various sports. Sex education classes are now fairly common at the high school and college level. Students are taught human anatomy and the mechanics of sexual functioning. But with rare exceptions, nowhere are they instructed on aspects of sexual failure. Many are not aware that it can occur, and even if they are, they assume that it is something that will happen to someone else.

This simple lack of knowledge is one of the major factors contributing to inadequate sexual performance. The situation may even be worsened by the damaging myths perpetuated not only by parents but by physicians. Young men may pass grossly erroneous information on to each other. Art Buchwald has satirized this situation well:

> I had no formal sex education when I was a student . . . we got all our sex education at the local candy store after 3 o'clock. The information was dispensed by thirteen year olds who seemed to know everything there was to know on the subject, and we eleven and twelve year olds believed every word they told us . . . for example . . . the method of kissing a girl on the mouth determined whether she would become pregnant or not. Every time I kissed a girl after that I sweated for the next nine months. . . . When I turned thirteen I became an instructor myself and passed on my knowledge to eleven and twelve year olds at the same candy store. . . . I was amazed with how much authority I was able to pass on the facts of life as I knew them. . . . We were all emotional wrecks before we got to high school.[4]

The Goal of This Book

Couples who are involved in a sexual crisis should not try to ignore it, deny it, or hope that it will disappear by itself, because it will not. Nor should they assume that there is no remedy for their particular problem. On the contrary, most forms of sexual inadequacy can be dealt with. The key to their solution is knowledge. It is the goal of this book to shed light on the serious problem of impotence and related sexual disorders in the hope that affected couples will understand how to begin making their sexual lives happier, more rewarding, and crisis-free.

It is unfortunate when a male does have sexual difficulties, but it is even more of a tragedy when either he or his female partner assumes that nothing can be done about it.

CHAPTER II
WHAT IS IMPOTENCE?

Definitions might be good things if only we did not employ words in making them.

—Rousseau

In its simplest terms, potency refers to the ability to achieve an erection that permits the introduction of the penis into the vagina and culminates in ejaculation and orgasm. Note that the frequency of intercourse is not part of the definition. A person who has intercourse successfully but only occasionally is not impotent.

Medical authorities divide impotence into primary and secondary forms. Primary impotence refers to the rare male who has never had an erection in his life. In secondary impotence, which comprises the majority of cases, a male has had erections and engaged in successful intercourse in the past, but currently his erectile ability is significantly reduced or absent.

In order to understand disorders of male sexual function, certain terms need to be defined. Ejaculation refers to the projection of semen. This is caused by contraction of muscular tissue within the penis and pelvis. Orgasm occurs at the culmination of the sexual act and is a pleasurable sensation representing both a physical and psychological response to ejaculation. Disorders of ejaculation, including uncontrollable ejaculation and failure to ejaculate, are not, strictly speaking, a part of impotence. But either of these conditions represents inadequate sexual performance and may lead to an impotent state.

Impotence and sterility are commonly confused terms. Sterility is the inability to have children and is often due to a lack of production of a sufficient number of normal living sperm. A sterile man may be able to have good erections. An impotent man, on the other hand, may produce sperm of normal quality but may not be able to impregnate his partner because he cannot achieve an erection sufficiently strong to permit successful intercourse.

It is also important to differentiate between impotence and decreased libido. While impotence refers to the inability to achieve an erection, decreased libido denotes diminishing interest in sexual activity or, more simply, a dwindling sex drive. It is not uncommon to find men who believe that they are impotent describing their problem as a lack of interest in sexual activity. Typically, a male who has previously been sexually successful states that something is wrong because he just hasn't thought about sexual activity for several months. Nothing seems to stimulate him. Very often the individual is engaged in a high-pressure job that is making him excessively fatigued or leaving him no time to spend with his female partner. He thinks that he's impotent, but in fact, if he were to try sexual intercourse at the appropriate time, in the appropriate setting, and with the appropriate female partner, he would not have difficulty performing.

Impotence and inadequate sexual performance may take many forms. For example, a male may be able to achieve an erection and begin intercourse, but the penis may become soft before completion of the act.

F. D., a fifty-year-old attorney, noticed a change in his sexual ability approximately three months before seeking medical attention. His past history was not unusual, and he had not experienced prior difficulties with intercourse. However, recently he had noticed that while his erections started out in normal fashion, the penis seemed to soften upon attempted insertion into the vagina. Initially, he attributed this to a state of physical fatigue, but when it occurred persistently, he sought advice. His female partner was very aware of the difficulty because the sexual act did not last long enough for her to have an orgasm.

Some males find that they are unable to ejaculate despite vigorous thrusting.

S. N., a sixty-two-year-old male, complained that he was unable to complete the sexual act because "nothing comes out." His sexual appetite was normal and there was no difficulty achieving an erection, but semen did not spurt out as usual. No matter what coital position was used, he could not ejaculate.

Very often an erection is achieved but the ejaculation cannot be controlled and comes too soon to permit penetration of the vagina.

M. R., a twenty-one-year-old male, had only recently lost his virginity and was having sexual relations with a female of his own age who had considerably more experience. To his great embarrassment, he seemed to become so sexually excited that he would ejaculate either just before vaginal penetration or shortly thereafter. He was chagrined and felt certain that his girl friend believed he was not a complete man.

Certain males may be able to achieve an erection only when gazing at pornographic material or in complete privacy. However, these individuals cannot perform with a female partner.

A. N., a thirty-one-year-old male, had been raised in a strict religious setting in which sexual activities were frowned upon. Masturbation was not an acceptable part of his society. He related to his physician that he had no trouble achieving an erection when he saw pornographic material either in a magazine or a movie, but that he had not been able to consummate his recent marriage because of failure to get a sufficient erection.

Some men can function sexually with a prostitute or other woman for whom they have no emotional feelings, but find themselves impotent with a woman for whom they truly care.

S. R., a forty-seven-year-old male, never married, had recently begun dating an attractive woman who worked in his office. He respected her greatly, and they developed a close emotional relationship. He regarded her as a very special person. His sexual history was normal, and on one occasion, five years earlier, he had gotten a woman pregnant and she had had an abortion. On his first occasion in bed with his new female companion, he could not achieve an erection. Despite her great patience and great encouragement, intercourse did not occur.

Certain males can only perform if they fantasize that they are with a different woman.

M. M., a thirty-eight-year-old male, had been married for seven years and was the father of two children. Recently his sexual interest in his wife seemed to decline, and intercourse usually occurred only if she initiated it. Erections became increasingly difficult to attain and maintain until it reached the point where M. M. would close his eyes during intercourse and imagine that he was in the arms of his secretary.

Some males cannot understand why at some times they are able to perform well sexually, yet at others, are unable to perform at all.

N. R., a forty-four-year-old male, directed a highly successful business that he had founded. He had his emotional ups and downs, which seemed to be connected with how well his business was running. He enjoyed sexual activity, and he and his wife had intercourse two to three times a week. After a six-week period in which he was unable to achieve an erection, he sought medical attention. During this same period of time, he was in the midst of a lawsuit that threatened his company's financial position.

Some individuals who have repeatedly failed to get an erection despite the most opportune circumstances declare that they are not really interested in sex and won't try again.

B. F., a sixty-one-year-old executive, was forced by his female partner to see a physician because of impotence. When they were interviewed, the woman complained that her partner was not interested in sex at all. In private, B. F. disclosed that he had attempted intercourse with a young secretary from his office and with another woman whom he had met at a recent business convention. Both of these women were unusually attractive and most receptive to his advances. Yet he had been unable to achieve an erection with either of them. He had now failed with three different women in a very short period of time. His sexual drive had waned, and he expressed a general disinterest in sexual activity.

All of the above are examples of impotence or inadequate sexual performance. While some men can't get an erection, others complain of not being able to maintain one long enough to complete the sexual act. Some males can't ejaculate during intercourse, and others do so too quickly. Certain men can function sexually only with some women, but not with others. Some can achieve an erection and ejaculate through self-stimulation, but not with a female partner. Others seem to have lost their sex drive. Despite some differences, all of the above problems are variations on a common theme: a lack of satisfactory sexual functioning.

CHAPTER III
A LOOK AT THE PAST

---

*Not to know what has been transacted in
former times is to continue always a child.*

—Cicero

The problem of impotence is age-old. It is well documented in historical and literary writings.[1,2,3] Sexual anxiety in childhood as a cause of impotence in adult life was recorded in Greek mythology. King Phylacus asked his physician, Melampus, to cure his son, Iphiculs, who was suffering from impotence. Melampus discovered that in childhood Iphiculs had seen his father brandishing a bloodstained gelding knife. He became terrified that he was going to be castrated, and it was this fright that allegedly accounted for his impotence in later years. By carefully pointing out how his fear had developed, Melampus was able to cure Iphiculs of his impotence.

A passage from Genesis (20:1) has been interpreted by some as a description of how Abimelech became impotent as a divine punishment for taking Abraham's wife: "But God came to Abimelech in a dream by night and said to him, behold, thou art a dead man, for the woman which thou has taken; for she is a man's wife."

Beginning in the Middle Ages and for many years thereafter, impotence was believed to be a curse inflicted by witches. A dramatic example of this concerns Don Carlos (1661–1700), who was the last of the Spanish Hapsburgs. He failed to give Spain an heir; this later led to the War of the Spanish Succession. Don Carlos was described as physically weak and of limited mental ability as a result of many generations of inbreeding. Despite two marriages, he was unable to produce the vitally needed heir to assure continuation of his family line. It was believed that he was impotent. Public opinion determined that Carlos was bewitched. Exorcisms were performed, but his impotence persisted to the end of his life. When he died, so did the Spanish Hapsburgs.

Some important literary figures were afflicted with sexual difficulties. For instance, George Bernard Shaw's sexual life is controversial. While some believe he was promiscuous, others believe he was impotent. Some have attributed the latter to homosexual tendencies that caused Shaw sexual anxiety. His own marriage was described as one of "contractual sexlessness."

Rousseau related an episode of impotence that occurred when he was with an attractive prostitute. "Suddenly, instead of the fire that devoured me, I felt a deathly cold flow through my veins; my legs trembled; I sat down on the point of fainting and wept like a child."

Twenty-three hundred years ago, Hippocrates noted that a preoccupation with business as well as a lack of female attractiveness could cause impotence. And the Hindus warned that impotence could follow an encounter with a female a man had found distasteful.

The *Malleus Maleficarum*, a manual dealing with witchcraft published in 1488, discussed the causes and treatment of impotence. Remedies included the use of splints and special herbs.

Many societies devised their own unique methods of treating impotence. In Europe, "phallic foods" were once popular; these included fresh eggs, lobsters, leguminous plants, French beans, and oysters. Years ago, Egyptians regarded the crocodile as a phallic symbol. Some actually ate the crocodile's penis in order to increase their potency.

Treatments that were in vogue only forty years ago now seem rather curious. Metal rods, which were first either heated or cooled, were passed into the penis in order to alleviate any inflammation therein. Another form of therapy consisted of electrical shocks that were applied to the testicles. Some doctors advocated an operation to tighten the muscles beneath the scrotum· which were considered to be weak. A most interesting apparatus was the penile splint. This peculiar-looking device allowed the male to penetrate the female even when his penis was soft. Today none of these methods is thought to be of any use.

CHAPTER IV
UNDERSTANDING ERECTIONS

There may be some things better than sex, and some things may be worse, but there is nothing exactly like it.

—W. C. Fields

In order to understand impotence, it is necessary to understand the mechanism of erections.

An erection is a reflex involving little voluntary control. Man unfortunately cannot command himself to have an erection. On the other hand, sometimes one occurs at an inopportune time; every man at one time or another has had to button his raincoat or turn over onto his belly at the beach in order to conceal an unexpected erection.

To achieve an erection, stimulation, either physical or mental, is required. This stimulation may be tactile, such as feeling a breast; visual, such as seeing the unclothed body of his partner; auditory, such as responding to erotically sensuous music; or even olfactory, such as smelling a perfume. A man may have sexually stimulating thoughts that also result in an erection. All of these are examples of psychogenic stimulation.

On the other hand, an erection may be reflexogenic. This is brought about by stimulation of the penis, testicles, or scrotum.

One of the major contributions of William H. Masters and Virginia E. Johnson has been to detail the physiology of the male sexual response.[1] Their observations were based on studying more than 300 men whose ages ranged from the early twenties to the late eighties and who participated in a total of over 2,500 sexual encounters. Masters and Johnson noted four phases of sexual response. In the excitement phase, blood rushes into the penis faster than it is drained away, so that an erection occurs. The rigidity of the penis thus comes from blood that circulates throughout the body being directed into the erectile tissue of the penis (the corpora cavernosa). This tissue is like a sponge that accepts blood and becomes very firm. Routing the blood to the penis requires a normal nervous system. With sexual excitement, the testicles draw upward into the scrotum and the opening at the end of the penis begins to enlarge. In some men, the nipples become firm and erect. The muscles of the legs and arms may become tense, and the rate of breathing increases.

In the second phase of sexual response, the plateau phase, the head of the penis, known as the glans, increases in diameter. The testicles are maximally elevated within the scrotum. Muscular tension is increased and there is involuntary contraction of the facial muscles, so that the male actually appears to frown. A fine red rash may develop over the neck, face, and upper chest. A few drops of seminal fluid may be released from the end of the penis.

During the third phase, the orgasmic phase, the male experiences a feeling that ejaculation is imminent and inevitable. At this time, the secretions from several glands, including the testicles and prostate, are deposited in the urethra. This results in the man's experiencing a sensation that semen is about to be released. As the muscles of the urethra and penis contract, the opening to the bladder closes, so that the seminal fluid mixed with sperm shoots forth from the penis. A volume of one to five cubic centimeters is ejected one to two feet out of the end of the penis. The rate of breathing may increase to more than thirty breaths per minute. The mouth usually remains open. The heart rate shoots up to between 100 and 180 beats per minute, and the blood pressure may rise significantly. At the time of orgasm there may be involuntary contractions of the muscles of the legs, buttocks, and feet.

It has often been assumed that the male's perception of orgasm is different from the female's. However, one study indicates that the written descriptions of orgasm are very similar for both sexes.[2] When these descriptions were studied by physicians, pyschologists, and medical students, not one expert could tell which had been written by men and which by women.

The following comments about what an orgasm feels like were made by both males and females. Note that it is not possible to determine which sex is talking.

A sudden feeling of lightheadedness followed by an intense feeling of relief and elation. A rush. Intense muscular spasms of the whole body. Sense of euphoria followed by deep peace and relaxation.

Feels like tension building up until you think it can't build up any more, then release. The orgasm is both the highest point of tension and the release almost at the same time. Also feeling contractions in the genitals. Tingling all over.

Obviously, we can't explain what it feels "like" because it feels "like" nothing else in human experience. A poetic description may well describe the emotions that go with it, but the physical "feeling" can only be described with very weak mechanical terminology. It is a release that occurs after a period of manipulation has sufficiently enabled internal, highly involuntary spasms that are pleasurable due to your complete involuntary control (no control).

It's like shooting junk on a sunny day in a big, green, open field.

I really think it defies description by words. Combination of waves of very pleasurable sensations and mounting of tensions culminating in a fantastic sensation and release of tension.

Orgasm gives me a feeling of unobstructed intensity of satisfaction. Accompanied with the emotional feeling and love one has for another, the reality of the sex drive, and our culturally conditioned status on sex, an orgasm is the only experience that sends my body and mind into a state of beautiful oblivion.

Tension builds to an extremely high level—muscles are tense, etc. There is a sudden expanding feeling in the pelvis and muscle spasms throughout the body followed by release of tension. Muscles relax and consciousness returns.

A building of tension, sometimes, and frustration until the climax. A tightening inside, palpitating rhythm, explosion, and warmth and peace.

A feeling where nothing much else enters the mind other than that which relates to the present, oh sooo enjoyable and fulfilling sensation. It's like jumping into a cool swimming pool after hours of sweating turmoil. "Ahhh! Relief!" What a great feeling it was, so ecstatically wild and alright!

A feeling of intense physical and mental satisfaction. The height of a sexual encounter. Words can hardly describe a feeling so great.

The fourth phase of sexual response described by Masters and Johnson is called resolution. Following ejaculation, the penis softens as blood drains out of it. During that time a male cannot achieve another erection despite the most vigorous stimulation. The length of this period varies from man to man. Hence the female should expect and the male accept the fact that he may not be able to perform again for a certain amount of time. There is no doubt that this period increases with age, and that older individuals will require more time than younger ones to achieve the next erection.

During resolution, the scrotum relaxes and the testicles

descend. The skin flush disappears, and the man may perspire lightly, particularly on the palms and soles.

Most men do not realize that virtually every normal male has approximately four to five erections a night, each lasting between fifteen and twenty-five minutes. During these erections, emission and ejaculation do not generally occur, though with stimulation, such as an exciting sexual dream, they may. This results in a nocturnal emission, or "wet dream."

Wilhelm Stekel wrote that "the capacity for erection begins on the day of birth and extinguishes with death." [8] It is not well known that babies, as well as very old men, may have erections. Newborn males have been noted to have an erect penis in the delivery room. And female babies may have vaginal lubrication. A physiological reason for these observations has yet to be determined.

We have made great strides in understanding erections, and the information gleaned from the laboratory is helping us increasingly in treating erectile failure.

CHAPTER V
HOW OFTEN DOES THE AVERAGE MAN HAVE INTERCOURSE?

A reasonable man needs only to practice moderation to find happiness.

—Goethe

Many impotent males and their partners misunderstand greatly how often other couples have intercourse. Their misconceptions may impose further unnecessary pressures upon an already frustrated and discouraged man. Therefore, information concerning frequency of intercourse of normally functioning males may be beneficial.

No one is really certain how many times a week the average male has intercourse. Statistics are difficult to collect, since many people are reluctant to provide this information, and much of that which has been obtained may be exaggerated. Disraeli summed up the dilemma of numbers in an address to Parliament in which he said, "Gentlemen, there are three kinds of lies—lies, damned lies, and statistics." However, some data are available that are accurate enough to provide guidelines for the interested male and female.

The frequency of sexual intercourse varies with age. As we would expect, younger groups tend to be more sexually active than older groups. For example, one study showed that up to age thirty, approximately 44 percent of all men have intercourse three to four times a week, and at least 30 percent have intercourse one to two times a week. Between the ages of fifty and sixty only

5 percent have intercourse three to four times a week, and 16 percent have it one to two times a week. In the eighth decade, less than 1 percent have intercourse three to four times a week, and less than 5 percent, one to two times a week. These data are taken from a study by Dr. Carl Pearlman. They are presented in more detail in the following tables.[1]

TABLE 1

FREQUENCY OF INTERCOURSE BY ALL MALE PATIENTS SURVEYED

Age	Number of patients	Times per week			Times per month			
		3–4	1–2	1	3	2	1 or less	None
20	9	44.4%	33.3%	11.1%	—	—	11.1%	—
20–29	323	43.6%	28.5%	17.6%	2.2%	4.0%	1.6%	2.5%
30–39	609	26.0%	29.1%	25.3%	3.6%	8.7%	5.4%	0.2%
40–49	571	14.0%	27.3%	27.3%	4.9%	12.4%	9.4%	4.7%
50–59	530	5.5%	16.2%	26.2%	4.1%	17.0%	19.3%	11.3%
60–69	472	0.8%	5.7%	18.4%	2.1%	13.7%	24.0%	35.6%
70–79	249	0.4%	3.6%	6.4%	1.2%	8.4%	20.9%	59.0%
80+	41	—	2.4%	2.4%	—	2.4%	7.3%	85.1%

Many people believe that single men are more sexually active than married ones, and that they are engaged in sexual activity whenever possible. However, Dr. Pearlman's study indicates that in fact married men are more active sexually. Between the ages of twenty and twenty-nine, 45 percent of married men have intercourse three to four times a week, while only 12 percent of single men have intercourse this often. Interestingly, divorced men are more sexually active at those same ages than either single or married men, as the following tables demonstrate.

TABLE 2

FREQUENCY OF INTERCOURSE BY MARRIED MALES

Age	Number of patients	Times per week			Times per month			
		3–4	1–2	1	3	2	1 or less	None
20	7	57.0%	43.0%	—	—	—	—	—
20–29	305	45.2%	29.6%	18.3%	0.9%	4.0%	0.3%	2.3%
30–39	592	26.5%	29.5%	25.6%	3.7%	8.4%	4.9%	1.2%
40–49	551	13.6%	28.1%	28.3%	5.0%	11.8%	8.9%	4.2%
50–59	517	5.2%	16.2%	27.1%	4.1%	17.4%	19.0%	11.0%
60–69	452	0.9%	6.0%	19.0%	2.2%	13.7%	25.0%	33.2%
70–79	238	0.4%	3.6%	6.7%	1.2%	8.8%	21.8%	57.0%
80+	37	—	2.7%	2.7%	—	2.7%	8.1%	83.7%

TABLE 3

FREQUENCY OF INTERCOURSE BY SINGLE MALES

Age	Number of patients	Times per week			Times per month			
		3–4	1–2	1	3	2	1 or less	None
20	2	—	50.0%	—	—	—	50.0%	—
20–29	16	12.5%	18.2%	12.5%	25.0%	6.8%	25.0%	—
30–39	5	—	—	20.0%	—	40.0%	40.0%	—
40–49	5	20.0%	—	—	—	40.0%	20.0%	20.0%
50–59	2	—	—	—	—	—	100.0%	—
60–69	6	—	—	16.6%	—	—	—	83.4%
70–79	2	—	—	—	—	—	—	100.0%

TABLE 4

FREQUENCY OF INTERCOURSE BY DIVORCED MALES

Age	Number of patients	Times per month			Times per week			
		3–4	1–2	1	3	2	1 or less	None
20–29	2	50.0%	—	—	—	—	—	50.0%
30–39	9	11.1%	22.2%	11.1%	—	11.1%	22.2%	22.2%
40–49	15	26.6%	6.7%	—	—	20.0%	26.6%	20.0%
50–59	9	22.2%	22.2%	—	11.1%	—	22.2%	22.2%
60–69	4	—	—	—	—	—	—	100.0%
70–79	2	—	—	—	—	—	—	100.0%

How Often Does the Average Man Have Intercourse?

In a very revealing survey published by *Playboy* magazine in October 1973, more than 2,000 people in twenty-four cities and suburban areas were interviewed.[2] The article showed that since Dr. Alfred Kinsey's epic report more than twenty-five years ago, there has been a general increase in the frequency of sexual intercourse.[3] In Kinsey's studies, the median frequency of sexual intercouse for married couples twenty-five years of age or younger was about 130 times a year, while more recent estimates have risen to approximately 154 times per year. For ages thirty-six to forty-five, the median frequency of sexual intercourse noted by Kinsey was 75 times a year, while more recently it has risen to 99. For married people beyond their mid-fifties, the median has increased from 26 to 49 times per year.

It is generally recognized that one's early sexual activity normally affects one's later sexual behavior. Generally speaking, men who engage in sexual intercourse at an early age tend to participate in sexual intercourse longer than those men who began their sexual activity later.

What is "too often" for one couple may be "too infrequent" for another. If a woman desires sexual intercourse nearly every day and her male partner is satisfied with having relations only twice a week, he may seem inadequate to her. On the other hand, another woman with a much lower sexual appetite might find intercourse twice a week to be too sexually demanding. It is when a couple's desires are widely divergent that the relationship is threatened. In his classic work *Psychopathia Sexualis*, Krafft-Ebing describes one man who

appeared, according to the statement of his wife, in the whole time of their married life covering a period of twenty-eight years, hypersexual, extremely libidinous, ever potent, in fact, insatiable in his marital relations. During coitus he became quite beastial and wild, trembled all over with excitement and panted heavily. This nauseated the wife who, by nature, was rather frigid, and rendered the discharge of her conjugal duty a heavy burden.[4]

It is truly impossible to state firmly what is the "normal" frequency of intercourse for couples. It is more important that both partners in a relationship be satisfied with the pattern of their sexual life.

CHAPTER VI
PSYCHOLOGICAL CAUSES
OF IMPOTENCE

---

*Body and Mind. We shall never get straight
till we leave off trying to separate these two
things. Mind is not a thing at all or, if it is,
we know nothing about it. It is a function
of the body. Body is not a thing at all or, if
it is, we know nothing about it. It is a function of the mind.*

—Samuel Butler

The causes of impotence are characteristically divided
into two broad categories: organic and psychological.
Generally speaking, organic impotence refers to those
cases of erectile failure that are due to physical causes.
Traditionally it has been taught that psychological problems accounted for 95 percent of all cases of impotence,
and that physical disorders were responsible for only 5
percent. More recently, however, some experts have stated
that physical problems may be associated with 50 percent
of all cases. In addition, it must be recognized that a
psychological reason can coexist with a physical one.

Once a male has been unable to achieve an erection,
the stage is set for repeated failures. During subsequent
attempts at intercourse, the impotent male becomes over-
anxious and fearful that he will not be able either to
attain or to sustain an erection. This extreme anxiety
actually inhibits the erectile process. The male thus develops a fear of failure, and a vicious cycle is established.

As the impotent male tries harder and harder, the likelihood that he will succeed continues to decrease.

The most important feature of psychological impotence is that it is not usually persistent. It may occur under certain conditions but disappear under others. For example, a man may be unable to achieve an erection with one female, but function perfectly normally with another. Or he may be unable to successfully penetrate a vagina, but on the other hand may have a firm penis during masturbation and enjoy ejaculation and orgasm. Or he may have erections during the day, aroused by pornographic material or sexual fantasies, but be unable to achieve them in the privacy of the bedroom, alone with his partner.

Several findings point to a psychological source of impotence. If a male awakens with erections or achieves an erection at night while he is asleep, his physical apparatus is intact. Likewise, if he can achieve an erection, ejaculate, and have an orgasm while masturbating, there is usually no physical reason for his failure to achieve an erection during attempted intercourse.

The most common psychological causes of impotence are discussed in this chapter.

Anxiety or Fear

In our present complex and rapid-paced society, there are many potential sources of anxiety or fear. One may experience anxiety concerning one's health, financial status, or job security. Many men fear they may not be able to bring their partner to orgasm and hence be rejected. Some men have a persistent fear of being punished for observing their parents having sexual intercourse when they were a child, though usually this observation was inadvertent and unintentional. Some men cannot accomplish intercourse successfully for fear of creating a pregnancy or contracting a venereal disease. This case history is one example:

Ben, a twenty-six-year-old male, had enjoyed many

sexual triumphs as a bachelor. He had always been able to achieve an erection and felt that he was especially talented in helping his partners reach orgasms. He was engaged for a period of seven months and was enjoying a normal sexual life with his fiancée, having intercourse approximately three times a week. One month prior to his wedding date and without any forewarning, he found himself unable to achieve an erection with his partner. There had been no change in his fiancée's sexual appetite, and his feelings toward her were as strong as ever. He was able to masturbate successfully with a firm penis. He was seen by a psychiatrist who determined that psychic conflict about an impending everlasting bond and the thought of sexual commitment to a single partner for the rest of his life were responsible for his problem. He was married as planned, and after two months of counseling, he was able to resume normal sexual functioning.

The Dhat syndrome is an example of the way extreme anxiety about the emission of semen may result in impotence.[1] This syndrome has been seen in patients attending psychiatric clinics in northern India. People suffering from this neurosis develop severe anxiety and hypochondriasis because of nocturnal emissions (wet dreams), and they may become impotent.

The development of this syndrome is explained by the fact that in India seminal fluid is regarded as an elixir of life. Semen is considered to be a precious material that is formed from blood. The belief exists that it takes forty meals to give rise to one drop of blood, and that forty drops of blood will give rise to one drop of bone marrow. Forty drops of bone marrow give rise to one drop of semen. Therefore, a single ejaculation is regarded as the loss of a significant amount of energy.

Men suffering from the Dhat syndrome seek medical help in the hope that their nocturnal emissions can be halted.

Aversion to Female Genitalia, and
Female Unattractiveness

Some men are repulsed by the appearance of the female's external genitalia. Others feel they are inserting their penis into an excretory orifice, which of course is not the case anatomically, since urine in the female is excreted through a separate channel. However, some men persist in feeling that sex is dirty and vulgar.

Steve, age twenty-five, was raised in a Midwestern rural setting by very religious parents. His father was a deacon at the local church, and his mother sang in the choir every Sunday. Steve was an only child, and the first time he left home for any significant duration was to attend college in a neighboring state. He had no sexual experience to speak of prior to leaving home. His first acquaintance with female anatomy was through pornographic magazines, which were frequently found in the dormitory. Initially, even browsing through these magazines caused Steve some feelings of anxiety and guilt. His peers boasted widely of frequent sexual encounters with girls.

At the library one evening, he met and was attracted to a young coed, and they soon began to see each other on a regular basis. Eventually they engaged in "petting," and she manually masturbated him. She did not understand why he did not attempt intercourse, but she did not initially confront him with this question. One evening she attempted to insert his erect penis into her vagina and to her bewilderment the erection rapidly faded. This episode was repeated the next evening, and Steve knew that he had a problem. He was ashamed and embarrassed and abruptly terminated the relationship. His partner did not understand Steve's difficulty, but since she had previously enjoyed sexual intercourse with several partners, she did not feel that she was in any way to blame. Steve eventually saw a psychiatrist at the college health center, and subsequent analysis revealed that he was a fastidious, compulsive young man who felt that the female genitalia were "private" and "unclean." He was a compulsive hand-washer and had a general fear of germs and infection.

Steve completed college very successfully from an academic standpoint, but at the time of graduation was still a virgin. He eventually sought psychiatric help again, but after several months, terminated his treatment.

Some men shun intercourse with a partner who has had a colostomy or a breast removed. Poor hygiene may also be a contributing factor, particularly if it involves the genitalia. Obesity in women is another factor men often cite as causing them to lose sexual interest. It is generally thought that obese women engage in less sexual activity than those whose weight is "normal."

The First Attempt

In the United States, the median age for the first episode of sexual intercourse for males is seventeen. Some individuals, of course, gain their first experience much earlier. Few boys will admit that they are still virgins after the age of sixteen.

Studies indicate that at least 20 percent of all males are unsuccessful in their first attempt at intercourse. The most common reasons for failure are the inability to maintain an erection, and uncontrollable ejaculation. Some of these individuals do not possess adequate knowledge of the female anatomy and are uncertain how to complete the sexual act. Often their only sexual information is derived from locker room conversation, or from friends who may be only slightly experienced. Because many of his peers boast of their sexual prowess and conquests, the young male who has not yet engaged in his first sexual act may develop unrealistic expectations about how he is to perform. Yet he does not really know what his partner expects of him, and is uncertain as to how she will react at the sight of his organ. Most young men (and old males as well) are grossly misinformed as to the normal length of the penis in its soft and erect states. Since a virgin is scorned in our culture, the inexperienced

49

young man is reluctant to seek advice from those who could really help him.

Most young men are very easily aroused by any sexual stimulation, but they know that their performance is dependent upon achieving and maintaining an erection sufficient to complete the sexual act. And even though the young man may achieve an erection with ease, he is often uncertain as to how to proceed, and hence loses his momentum. Often the setting in which the first sexual experience takes place is far less than ideal. The back seat of the car has been replaced by the bedroom, but very often it is located in his girl friend's home or in his dormitory, and in either place he may feel uncomfortable and tense. He may feel that speed is of the essence, since he is uncertain as to when an unexpected interruption may occur. If the male's first experience occurs with a prostitute, he may be overwhelmed by her experience or her demands. In addition, her mechanical approach may be sufficient to discourage him. Any of these factors may result in the young man's losing his erection and failing to penetrate his partner. While this experience is one that will never be forgotten, it is also one that is usually easily analyzed by the male, whose second sexual attempt may then be successful. Persistent failure usually necessitates professional counseling.

Warren, a seventeen-year-old high school senior with an excellent academic record and letters in both football and basketball, had everything going for him. He was one of the most popular boys in school and served as vice-president of his class. His good looks, combined with his athletic prowess, caught the attention of many girls. He had recently been dating a girl one year younger than himself and had made up his mind to attempt intercourse with her if given the opportunity. This would be his first coital experience. Prior to this time, he had masturbated with a firm erection and ejaculated without difficulty. He did not require pornographic material; fantasizing about sexual encounters was sufficient. Like many of his peers, he boasted of his sexual encounters when in fact he was a virgin. He did not look forward to Monday mornings when all the guys got together and recounted their weekend sexual escapades, but he kept up a good front. He worried that someone might detect his virginity.

When he and his girl friend were alone in her house one evening, their foreplay progressed and she was most willing to have intercourse. Both were unclothed. His girl friend clutched him tightly, obviously awaiting his next move, but to his astonishment he could not achieve an erection. Hoping that things would improve, he manually stimulated his partner; still his penis remained limp. His girl friend remained silent and did not understand what had gone wrong. The following Monday proved more painful than most as he listened to his fellow classmates brag about their Saturday night sexual experiences. He could not refrain from mentioning that he, too, had had a great time.

He lived with this dishonesty, but not easily. He had no one with whom he could discuss his problem. He knew this was something he could never talk about with his father, and there was no physician he felt he could confide in. He bought a book that seemed to be a sex manual but found nothing in it that explained his own failure.

Two weeks later, in the same setting, he again attempted intercourse and this time was able to penetrate, although he noted that the penis was not as firm as it was during masturbation. He did ejaculate, and his partner was satisfied. He felt considerably better about himself and looked forward to the Monday morning bull-session, when sexual stories were swapped.

In subsequent sexual encounters he developed a full erection, although he ejaculated shortly after penetration. He has since graduated from college and has had no further difficulty with erection. The first time he was ever able to discuss his former problem was during a counseling session in medical school.

Fear of Fatherhood

It is not uncommon for women to desire children earlier than their husbands. To many men, children will pose problems: loss of freedom, financial responsibilities, and resentment at the prospect of sharing the mother's affection with another. In addition, many women who work may leave their jobs when they become pregnant, and this may involve significant loss of income. With potential fatherhood on their minds, some men find that they cannot achieve an erection.

Ken, a thirty-year-old engineer, had been married for five years. He and his wife had engaged in premarital intercourse and still enjoyed an active sexual life, having relations approximately three times a week. Both were well educated and broad-minded. His wife was sexually responsive, and oral sex was a regular part of their repertoire. Both had agreed that children were not to be considered until after Ken had completed his formal training. Birth control pills were used as a means of contraception. At twenty-seven, Ken's wife felt that because of her age they should no longer delay having a child.

Prior to marriage, Ken had never given much thought to having children, and by now he was somewhat set in his ways. He enjoyed his relationship with his wife and could really find no good reason to have a child. When his wife discontinued taking her birth control pills, he kept a mental record of her menstrual cycle. He then managed for several months to avoid sexual intercourse at the time of ovulation, when his wife could conceive. When she finally confronted him with this fact, he developed a new ploy, which was to masturbate before retiring. He reasoned that when he did have intercourse and ejaculate, the sperm count would be lower and the chances of conception would be markedly diminished. After failing to conceive, his wife insisted he see a urologist for an infertility evaluation. During their initial joint interview, his true feelings about having children were expressed and the infertility counseling was discontinued.

At home their relationship became more strained, and petty arguments developed. The frequency of intercourse decreased, and eventually Ken found that he had difficulty maintaining an erection. His wife viewed this as a conscious attempt to avoid the possibility of impregnation. However, Ken became very concerned as he realized that he was having difficulty attaining a firm penis even when his wife wasn't ovulating. After repeated failures he avoided any attempts at intercourse. Their relationship rapidly deteriorated and the marriage ended in divorce.

The fear of causing a pregnancy may also cause impotence in the unmarried male, who usually is aware of the unfortunate consequences of a pregnancy occurring out of wedlock. His fear may result in anxiety sufficient to prevent erections. However, recently many single males have dismissed any concern about the possibility of their partner's becoming pregnant because of the ease with which an abortion may be obtained.

Inhibition

A male who is sexually inhibited has usually acquired this trait as a result of strong religious beliefs, severe parental influence, or self-imposed restraint. Walker and Strauss, in *Sexual Disorders in the Male*, commented upon culturally determined sexual inhibitions:

There is a disposition on the part of some married couples to feel that while certain methods of lovemaking are right and proper, others are illegitimate and degrading. It is chiefly because the British (and presumably the Americans) pay great respect to convention that their method of lovemaking rarely departs from a certain accepted model. But love has not always been so conventional. In the Kama Sutra, an early Hindu treatise on sexual relationships, we read of at least seven different ways of kissing, eight varieties of touch, eight playful bites, four methods of stroking the body with the hands and eight sounds that may be emitted whilst doing so.[2]

One of the great examples of moral inhibition concerns the philosopher Goethe, who himself experienced an episode of impotence and perceptively recognized its cause. Goethe wrote in his diary that he once was returning home from the city when a wheel of his carriage broke. This necessitated spending the night at a local inn, where he was attracted to a beautiful young waitress who later that evening visited his room. She informed Goethe that she was a virgin but was willing to go to bed with him, at which point Goethe's great desire was abruptly replaced by an overwhelming sense of morality that rendered him impotent. Goethe had never before had any difficulty in coitus with his wife. He wrote in his diary that "if a demon approaches us and tempts us, something happens and the virtue is preserved."[3]

Occupational Difficulties

Our society is strongly oriented toward job success. Promotion means increased power, income, and prestige. Most men strive to succeed in their career, and reaching the top is always cause for celebration. Ambitious men are competitive and set high goals for themselves. If these goals are not attained, depression and loss of self-esteem may result. The depression that follows affects a man's entire life, including his sexual functioning. His interest in sexual activity may actually disappear, and even if he does not lose his desire, he may lose his ability to have an erection.

Because of their failure, many men cannot face their wives, and so turn to other women in an attempt to regain their self-confidence. However, to their surprise, they may find themselves impotent with their new partner as well. This is because they are really suffering from a generalized depression.

Alvin had been married for seventeen years and had

performed without any difficulty before he became impotent. He and his wife had three children. They had intercourse approximately two times a week, and she seemed generally satisfied, though she reached orgasm only sporadically.

Alvin had worked in the personnel office of a large utility company ever since his graduation from college. He was assistant to the director of his department, and all signs pointed to his assuming that position when his boss retired. To everyone's surprise, he was passed over and the position was filled from outside the company. Soon after, Alvin's interest in his wife waned and he began seeing a secretary in his office. They had sexual relations several times before she broke off the affair. Following this, he was unable to achieve an erection with his wife. She became depressed and sought advice from her gynecologist, who recommended sexual counseling. Alvin has thus far refused to seek treatment. He and his wife continue living together, although they have essentially no sexual life.

Homosexuality

Another cause of impotence is homosexuality. Some men have had sexual experiences only with other men. On occasion, some of these individuals have tried to have a heterosexual experience and have found themselves unable to attain an erection. Some bisexual men who have predominantly homosexual tendencies find it increasingly difficult to have intercourse with a female. These same individuals have no difficulty when engaging in sexual activity with another man.

John, a thirty-eight-year-old male, was married for approximately sixteen months and successfully engaged in sexual intercourse. His wife enjoyed her sexual experiences and was able to have an orgasm most of the time. John, who had had one homosexual experience while a teenager at camp, became involved with another male, and they developed an intense relationship. On an average of one to two times a week, he met his lover and they engaged in fellatio and anal intercourse. Gradually he found himself unable to achieve an erection with his wife. However, with his new male companion, he could do so. Despite six months of psychotherapy, he was unable to resume his normal heterosexual orientation and was divorced. He now lives with his male lover.

Sexual Trauma

A male who has committed rape or incest, or perhaps has indulged in an extramarital affair, may become impotent because of underlying guilt. Also, a male who may have been abused sexually early in life may have difficulty. Careful questioning readily brings out the association between adverse sexual experience and impotence. But although the impotent male may recognize the relationship between the two, successful treatment may take a long time.

George, age forty-seven, was a bricklayer who was referred for psychiatric help because of a psychosis. He had many severe problems, one of which was sexual functioning. Delving into his past revealed that he was raised essentially by his mother from the age of four, when his father left home. He had no brothers or sisters. George recalled his mother bathing him even when he was eleven years old. She spent a good deal of time washing his genitalia. He recalled having an erection during one bath. His mother pretended not to notice, but continued washing his penis. This became a common occurrence, and one evening his mother, who apparently had been drinking, came into his bedroom and began to massage his whole body. To his embarrassment he had an erection and his mother proceeded to mount his erect penis and insert it into her vagina. This happened only once, and following this his mother never bathed him again. There were no further episodes of sexual exploitation.

George had never married and had not gone out socially with a woman for fifteen years. In his early twenties, he had attempted intercourse twice but could not get an erection on either occasion. He was frightened of masturbation and had essentially no sexual outlet. While he was bowling one evening, a friend boasted of a pleasurable sexual experience he had had with a prostitute the week before. For several days this preyed upon George's mind. Finally, one night after he had had several drinks, he paid a visit to the same bordello.

It was a disastrous experience for him. Having paid the fee, he was taken to a small, dingy bedroom, where the prostitute abruptly disrobed. In a very businesslike voice, she instructed him to take off his pants and proceeded to wash his penis with soap and water. In bed, things went from bad to worse. George could not get an erection, even with oral stimulation. The prostitute made a series of belittling remarks and told him to either "get it up or get out." George struck her in the face, got dressed, and left.

The next day, he argued with his foreman and attempted to strike him. He was referred to the company doctor and eventually to a psychiatrist. He has been undergoing treatment for one year, and his prognosis is uncertain.

Boredom

It is human nature to become bored when one repeats the same thing over and over. Few people will reread the same book or see the same movie or paint the same picture again and again. We do not like to eat the same food day after day, or to wear the same clothing repeatedly. So it is not surprising that sexual intercourse repeated in the same way, in a mechanical fashion, becomes uninteresting. If there is not a personal and emotional commitment between the male and female partners, sexual contact may become not only boring but distasteful.

Underlying many cases of impotence is simple boredom with sexual relations. A typical history involves a couple who may have enjoyed sexual activity prior to marriage and for some time after marriage. After several years they find that their sexual activities are ritualized without any variation in pattern. The sexual act has become automatic and lacking in feeling. The female complains that her male partner does not display enough romantic effort, and that he expects her always to be sexually responsive at bedtime. Intercourse usually occurs at the same time, in the same place, and the same way. Its excitement and fun have disappeared. The partners will not discuss the problem with each other, and don't attempt to inject into sex any variation that might revive their interest. This may occur even in a relationship where strong feelings of love and devotion exist.

Jack, age forty-four, was married to Karen, age forty-three, when they sought counseling for their sexual problems. They had been married for thirteen years and had two children. Jack complained that "things just aren't the same." During intercourse his penis failed to attain its usual hard state, and although penetration was possible and ejaculation did occur, the act didn't seem as pleasurable as it once was. Karen complained that Jack did not seem as interested in her and that the frequency of coitus had decreased to between two and three times a month.

The couple had previously had intercourse two to three times a week, and almost without exception it had involved a minimum of foreplay. Jack would assume the superior position and ejaculate rather quickly after penetration. Karen had orgasm less than 10 percent of the time. This pattern of sexual activity had been going on for three years before Jack saw his family doctor with rather vague and general complaints, all of which pointed to the fact that he was depressed. Among other things, he was referred for sexual therapy. He and his wife subsequently entered group therapy sessions. These meetings revealed that other couples had similar difficulties, and suggestions were made that would introduce variations into their stale sexual habits. Jack and Karen have since made a favorable adjustment.

Declining interest in sexual activity may begin at any time, but for many couples it begins within a few years after marriage. Frequently the problem is sublimated as they both focus their attention on child rearing. Gradually, partners who are disinterested in sexual activity develop devices to prevent a potential encounter. There are easy ways to avoid going to bed at the same time and thus reduce the likelihood of intercourse. For example, a male may stay up late to finish a project, or a woman may decide that she wishes to finish a book or watch a television program. One partner may watch a program until the other drifts off to sleep, and thus the opportunity for lovemaking is lost. Johnny Carson has been quoted as saying that "we're more effective than birth control pills." The experience in a West Virginia city attests to this. Early in 1968, a strike halted television transmission by coaxial cable and all television programs were off the air. In 1969 the birth rate was triple that of the previous years, thus suggesting that sexual activity had likewise increased during the period of the television blackout.[4]

Some couples may eventually have intercourse only once or twice a year, and usually these encounters do not provide significant satisfaction. In these relationships, which have been termed "sexless" marriages, sexual activity is seemingly unimportant. This does not necessarily mean that the relationship is unstable, since if both partners share the same attitude about sex, there is no reason why they cannot live together harmoniously.

Men express dissatisfaction with their sexual relationship at home more frequently than women do. This is in part because of the male viewpoint on sex. Many men consider it a challenge to "conquer" a woman in bed. When victory has been won, their interest wanes, since the challenge is no longer present. Their emotional involvement in the sex act is diminished. Studies show that women tend to romanticize sex more than men, and have a stronger emotional commitment to both the sexual act and their partner. Thus, intercourse is often more rewarding for women and their interest in it does not diminish so easily. Often each partner will seek his or her own solution, and may end up involved in an extramarital affair or group sexual activity.

Many suggestions have been made on how to counteract the problem of boredom. These include such things as varying coital positions, trying sexual intercourse at different times of the day (such as on a lunch break, if it is feasible), and taking short vacations to get away from the routine of daily living. Most men feel rejuvenated and become more sexually aggressive when they are away from home with their female partner. Even a weekend in a motel may prove refreshing. The female partner may desire more romantic efforts on the part of her male partner. She may also be more stimulated if the period of foreplay is increased.

Retribution

Some men harbor an unconscious desire to punish their female partner, and preventing her from enjoying the pleasures of intercourse and orgasm is one way to do so. Very often, psychotherapy is necessary to uncover the male's motivation. If treatment is not undertaken, the relationship usually dissolves.

The Nonencouraging or Unresponsive Female

Many books are available that describe how a woman can maximize her sexual pleasure, and it is not uncommon for women, like men, to discuss their orgasmic abilities with one another. This change in women's attitudes has not gone unnoticed by men. They now expect their wives to be sexually active, and many enjoy the fact that their female partner takes an aggressive role during foreplay and intercourse. However, not all women are sexually responsive. Analysis of some impotent men reveals that they are married to women whose sexual behavior can best be described as nonencouraging. These women promote such foreplay as kissing, but they discourage any stimulation of their genital area. They also exhibit a generalized repulsion toward the male genitals. Some hide their own enjoyment of sexual activity and display a generalized disinterest in all sexual matters. This type of female may believe that she is not responsible for helping her partner to achieve an erection, and that she should not have to provide him with any type of physical encouragement; he should be involved only in satisfying her. This type of woman may refuse to touch her partner's genitals, or if she does, it is in a nonerotic way.

If a male cannot arouse his wife, or if his wife simply does not seem to enjoy the sexual act, the man may feel incompetent. It becomes apparent that the woman is simply avoiding the sexual act; and her partner may respond with disappointment or anger. He may attempt to educate himself, either through books or by seeking professional help, so that he may acquire the ability to stimulate his wife. However, if he continues to meet with negative reactions, he may soon find that he has difficulty in attaining or maintaining an erection. He is now faced with a partner who does not seem to enjoy sex, and even if she does, he may believe that he is unable to fulfill her desires.

A woman who appears apathetic to sex or who is not sexually responsive is a common cause of male sexual dysfunction. If a male is having intercourse less frequently than he would like, and if, when he does have sexual relations, his partner appears disinterested, the stage is set for an extramarital affair.

Bob, age thirty-one, was a professional musician who had never been married. He had spent many years playing the drums in local night spots and was now traveling across the country with a well-known band. In addition, his band accompanied an established rock-and-roll group on their professional recordings. Bob had graduated from college with a degree in sociology, but had immediately embarked upon his musical career. He had engaged frequently in sexual intercourse, but usually while he was traveling, and he had never had a sustained relationship with one woman. He had been exposed to a variety of women, some older and some younger, and regarded himself as very well educated sexually. He knew and used most of the positions for coitus, engaged freely in oral sex, and had enjoyed anal intercourse on occasion.

Lori was a senior in college when she met Bob while the band was on a college tour. During the next six months, they went out on three or four occasions and had a somewhat platonic relationship. Lori was a virgin, and fully intended to refrain from intercourse until marriage. She was decidedly different from any girl that Bob had previously dated, and he found her intriguing. Since he had ample sexual outlets with other women, he never forced the issue of intercourse with her, and in fact rarely engaged in more than kissing and fondling. Eventually they became engaged, and were married six months later. Bob had never seriously given any thought as to whether he would marry a virgin, and as he thought about it, he realized that he liked the idea. In effect, Bob married a girl about whom he knew nothing sexually.

On their wedding night, the marriage was consummated, but not without some discomfort to Lori. Bob noted that she seemed rather passive during intercourse, but he attributed this to her lack of experience. Within the next month, Bob became aware that he always initiated any sexual encounter. Foreplay seemed one-sided, with Bob alone providing the stimulation. Lori herself avoided Bob's genitalia, and while she reluctantly permitted cunnilingus, she never entertained the thought of fellatio. She had once read a novel in which a male ejaculated into his female partner's mouth, but the whole idea was repugnant to her.

Bob soon became extremely disenchanted with his sexual life and began to notice that he had difficulty achieving a firm erection. While Lori was always receptive to his advances, she never encouraged sexual activity. Bob knew from his earlier experiences with other women that the problem lay with his wife. He thought back to his earlier encounters and realized that he enjoyed a woman who took the sexual initiative on occasion. He began to fantasize about being raped by a woman. Finally, while traveling out of town with the band while his wife remained at home, he had intercourse with a girl whom he had previously known. She had a good sexual appetite, and that evening Bob's sexual performance went without any difficulty and he enjoyed himself thoroughly. Some months later, his wife learned about the episode from one of Bob's fellow band members, and she confronted him with the facts. Lori seemed less concerned about the actual physical act that he had with another woman than about whether his love for her was waning.

The couple sought marital counseling, and it was apparent that Bob's feelings for Lori were extremely strong and that he was well satisfied except in the sexual sphere. This couple is currently in sex therapy.

Depression

Depression may be caused by a variety of factors. Disappointment over career limitations, the realization that marriage is no longer stimulating, or disagreement on how to raise the children all may be precipitating factors. Depression may affect many bodily functions, including sex, and erectile failure may result. Other signs of depression include loss of appetite, insomnia, weight loss, or a lack of interest in work.

Depression may be mild or severe. Many mild cases are associated with transient impotence. When the male's emotional state has improved, sexual functioning may also return to normal. Impotence associated with a deep depression lasts longer and is more difficult to treat. Antidepressive medication may be of benefit in such cases.

Pressure to Perform

Women's liberation has made waves in many areas, including the realm of sex. The woman's sexual role in our society has changed dramatically. At one time, women were supposed to be only passive participants in sex. It was their duty to satisfy their husband, and whether they enjoyed intercourse was not a matter of primary concern. Nowadays, women are regarded as equal partners in sex, and many are very much concerned with whether or not they have an orgasm.

Many men feel an increased responsibility to ensure that their female partner will be sexually satisfied. Unfortunately, some men feel that they have failed if their partner does not have an orgasm during every sexual encounter. While this is not an undesirable goal, it may be an unrealistic one. Some women are simply not capable of achieving an orgasm during every act of intercourse. Some men feel that they have failed if their partner does not reach climax, and believe that they themselves are inadequate. If a male develops severe feelings of inadequacy, he may become secondarily impotent. This results from his anxiety over whether or not his partner will be satisfied. Naturally, if he cannot achieve an erection, his female partner cannot achieve an orgasm, and a cycle of failure is established. It should be pointed out to these males that, while sex is something you do *with* a woman and not *to* her, it is not necessarily a sign of failure on the male's part if a woman does not achieve an orgasm every time.

Howard, a thirty-nine-year-old investment manager for a bank, had been married to Joy for two years. His previous marriage had ended in divorce. Howard was a hard worker and was rising rapidly within his organization. It was not uncommon for him to bring work home from the office and spend several hours a night in his study. His wife, age thirty-five, was a teacher at the local high school. Howard felt that he had a rather typical and satisfactory sexual life. He and Joy had intercourse two or three times a week; Sunday afternoon was a particularly favorite time. Howard was rather straightforward in his sexual approach. Foreplay was short, and a very brief period of manual stimulation of the vagina was followed by penetration and ejaculation within two minutes. During this time, his wife was responsive and seemed to enjoy intercourse, though in fact she did not reach an orgasm and had not since their marriage.

After reading several articles on female sexual functioning, Joy realized that her sexual life was less than satisfactory. At the time of her routine gynecological examination, she discussed this with her physician, who advised her that there was no reason she should not be able to have an orgasm. One Sunday afternoon after she and Howard had had relations, she expressed concern that she was not having an orgasm. Howard was surprised because he thought that he had been a superior sexual technician and had been doing all the right things and that therefore she should be satisfied. Instead of increasing the length of foreplay, he followed his own routine, but after ejaculation he continued physical thrusting in the hope that Joy would reach orgasm. This became an effort on his part, and he would actually count to himself, usually to 100, before admitting defeat. He had been used to feeling total physical relaxation after ejaculation, and now he found himself doing what he regarded as work rather than pleasure.

Joy soon became aware of how much additional thrusting Howard would do after he had ejaculated. Instead of relaxing, she began to feel under pressure to achieve an orgasm. When she was still unable to do so, Howard began to feel that he was an inadequate lover. His personal worth was being tested, and he could not perform. This was in marked contrast to his success on the job, and it was difficult for him to regard himself as a failure. Their frequency of intercourse decreased, and eventually Howard began to note that his penis became less firm when he had an erection. This was also apparent to Joy, but she did not remark on the matter. With the penis less erect, there was less clitoral stimulation, and sex was less enjoyable for Joy than before.

Howard now regarded every encounter as a challenge, and all spontaneity in his sexual performance was lost. Because of his increasing difficulty in achieving an erection, he berated Joy because she was no longer able to stimulate him successfully. After they had had an argument one evening, he angrily suggested that she try going to bed with someone else to see if he could do any better. Three months later she had intercourse with a fellow teacher from her school and did reach climax. When Howard found out, his ego was demolished, and further attempts at sexual intercourse were even less successful. Howard was already insecure, and now during intercourse he began to compare himself with Joy's previous lover. He felt certain that his penis was not as long as her lover's, and he soon became unable to attain an erection. He and Joy eventually separated.

It would be ideal if the female had an orgasm from penile stimulation during every act of intercourse. However, this is not the case. While most females can climax if the length of foreplay and vaginal penetration is sufficient for their own psychological and physical needs, certain females may have difficulty ever achieving orgasm. A few have never had the experience. Some physicians believe too much emphasis has been placed on the female climax during vaginal penetration.

Today the female orgasm has become to a man his last reassurance of manhood, his last proof of being needed, as a man, by his woman. This he must achieve at all odds, even if his woman does not know what an orgasm is, or is frigid, or responds mainly to masturbation—no matter: he must be able to make her reach orgasm in intercourse, or he will feel frustrated and castrated not only in a purely sexual sense, but in the widest meaning of the term, as a man. Hence, the incredible emphasis on the phenomenon which, in patriarchal times, was hardly even considered compatible with the dignity of a lady, much less a matter of consequence.[5]

Women should realize that the pressure on the male to perform may become so great that he may actually feign the orgasmic response. Some men who are able to manage vaginal penetration quickly lose their erection, and rather than admit that they are impotent, pretend to experience an orgasm. The illusion that they have completed the sexual act in a short period of time is more acceptable to them than letting their partner know that they are indeed impotent and never reach a climax.

Male Infertility

It has been estimated that nearly 15 percent of marriages in the United States are barren. And in perhaps an additional 10 percent of cases, more children are desired than the couple is able to have. Until recently, the responsibility for the failure to produce a child was placed upon the shoulders of the female. It is now recognized that in approximately one-half of all cases, the male has some abnormality or deficiency. Since our society still associates a manly image with reproductive capability, a man who is unable to impregnate a woman may find his self-esteem threatened. As time passes and conception does not occur, pressure upon him may build. His female partner may be keeping a temperature chart to indicate when she is ovulating each month. When the chart indicates that ovulation is taking place, the couple may attempt to have relations up to three times a day. This mechanical approach to insemination may result in extraordinary pressure upon an already tense male. He may well find himself unable to obtain an erection, penetrate, and ejaculate. Some males become frustrated and resentful over "sex on demand," a complaint our society has most often heard voiced by the female in the past.

The following case history documents this problem.

Mike, a thirty-four-year-old surgeon, had been married to Susan for seven years. For the first five years of their marriage they chose not to have children because he was busy with medical training. Susan used birth control pills. Having mutually arrived at a decision to have a child, they discontinued the pills. After six months and no pregnancy, Susan underwent a basic gynecological examination and was told that she was normal. At this time, she urged her husband to see a urologist for evaluation, but he refused. After six more months, during which time Susan had not yet become pregnant, Mike agreed to be evaluated and was found to be physically normal. A semen analysis was performed; it was normal. This reassured Susan, who now was determined to become pregnant.

At her insistence the frequency of sexual intercourse was increased to two to three times a day for the forty-eight-hour period before and after her presumed day of ovulation. While initially Mike had no difficulty in complying, he gradually found that it took longer and longer to achieve an erection upon these occasions. Additional pressure was added by the fact that the first relations of the day occurred in the morning, when both were on a rushed schedule to get to work. As erections become more and more difficult for Mike, his wife began to use more innovative stimulation techniques, which initially were helpful but eventually failed. Soon Mike was unable to achieve an erection at any time. Susan's hopes for a pregnancy were dashed and she became depressed. Mike's self-image was destroyed and he wondered if he would ever be able to function sexually again. He and his wife eventually underwent sexual behavior counseling and he is now able to achieve an erection, though another year has elapsed and his wife is still not pregnant.

While some men cannot respond to these demands with an erection, others may attain a normal erection but find that they cannot control ejaculation long enough for satisfactory vaginal penetration. Thus, insemination cannot occur.

Unfortunately, the type of case history recounted above is becoming more and more common. This is in part due to the fact that many young couples are now trying to plan their lives very carefully. Many wives are successful career women and do not wish to take much time away from their occupations. Hence, many even try to plan the month in which they will deliver to coordinate with their working schedules. The burden thus placed upon the male may become excessive, and many fail to function altogether.

Unfortunately, many men may try to regain their self-image through successful sexual functioning in an extramarital affair. And indeed, some men have found that their ability to have a successful erection returns when the pressure and anxiety have been removed. However, some of these same individuals then develop guilt feelings over their affair and become impotent once again.

Some couples decide to adopt when the male becomes impotent. They may feel a pregnancy is impossible, and their overwhelming desire to have a child drives them to an adoption agency. It is not uncommon to find that such a couple, after having adopted one or more children, may eventually have a pregnancy of their own. This is often associated with the male's renewed sexual ability once the pressure for performance has been relieved by the newly adopted child.

Cancer

It is easy to understand the shock sustained when a man learns that he has cancer. While many malignancies are curable, particularly in their early stages, the general public still equates the diagnosis with the death knell. A person's self-image usually is severely altered, so that one feels less self-reliant. Anxiety and depression are eventually followed by a sense of resignation. Throughout this period a male's general sexual desire may wane. Eventually, when an attempt at intercourse is made, erectile failure may occur. Most males believe that it is their underlying disease that is causing their sexual problem, when in fact it is more often the psychological reaction to the illness that is responsible. Even the fear of developing a malignancy is often enough to prevent successful sexual functioning.

Dave, a forty-four-year-old investment banker, complained of a recent onset of impotence. He had been married for fourteen years and was the father of three children. He enjoyed sexual intercourse an average of two times a week, and his wife enjoyed the sexual act, often having an orgasm.

Dave could not pinpoint the exact time his impotence began, but careful questioning by his urologist soon revealed that he began experiencing difficulty while he was undergoing evaluation for a rather unusual skin disorder. He had had several large skin lesions on his inner thighs and back and had sought a dermatological opinion. Consultation with several skin specialists had been required before a diagnosis was established. He had been told that he did not have a malignancy, but that in some individuals these types of lesions could herald the onset of a tumor. Dave was stricken with the realization that he had no control over the likelihood of his developing cancer. This was not easy for him to accept since he was a man who led a rather orderly and controlled life both at home and at work. Dave's sexual problem was correlated with poor performance in the investment business. In addition, he became depressed and short-tempered.

With the help of his urologist, Dave concluded that his performance failure was due to a general anxiety. This realization seemed to provide him with a brighter outlook, and he is currently planning to participate in sexual counseling along with his wife.

Kidney Failure

Until recently, patients with advanced kidney disease did not survive, and therefore their sexual functioning was not considered. Now, however, patients with no kidney function whatever can be kept alive by one of two means. A patient may undergo a kidney transplant or may be maintained on an artificial kidney machine. (The latter procedure is known as dialysis.) Using either of these methods, many patients can return to their jobs and resume a nearly normal social life. It is natural that these patients would wish to resume sexual activity. However, a large percentage of them are unable to do so. One study reveals that 59 percent of all male dialysis patients and 43 percent of all patients who have received a kidney transplant consider themselves partially or totally impotent.[6] Many male dialysis and transplant patients report that they never have intercourse. Before the development of their kidney failure, most of these patients had normal sex lives. It is not entirely clear why these male patients are unable to attain an erection, though certainly many emotional factors may play a role. Almost all of these patients have been through a long ordeal with chronic illness. Those on dialysis are aware that they are dependent on a machine for the rest of their lives, and men who have received a kidney transplant are faced with the possibility of failure of the transplanted organ. This kind of anxiety, or indeed any kind of anxiety over a major medical disorder, may result in sexual dysfunction.

Many men who are impotent try to ignore the problem by avoiding all attempts at intercourse. Some will say that they are too tired, and others feel that they are just too busy. Art Buchwald's satire entitled "Never on Monday Either" makes its own point:

The subject of sex in marriage is no longer taboo, and more and more institutes have been set up to help married couples find sexual happiness together.

Dr. Henrico Belladonna, who runs the Clinic of Marital Bliss in Spring Valley, told me, "One of the big discoveries we psychologists have made is that not all sexual problems in today's marriages can be attributed to fear. Our studies indicate that fear now ranks only second as a reason for sexual hang-ups."

"What is number one?" I asked.

"I'll show you," he said. "I have a couple in now. Why don't you go over and sit in that chair and observe what happens."

A man and wife entered nervously and the doctor asked them to be seated.

Dr. Belladonna waited for them to say something. Finally, the husband spoke up. "Doctor, we've come to your institute as a last resort. Our sex life seems to be on the rocks and we don't know what to do about it."

Dr. Belladonna said, "I would like to ask you a few questions. How often do you have relations each week?"

"Never," the wife said.

"Never?" Dr. Belladonna asked.

"It isn't that we don't want to," the husband said. "It's just that we don't seem to have the time any more."

"I see," said Dr. Belladonna. "Well, let's look into that. What's wrong with Monday night?"

"Oh," said the husband, "we can't do it on Mondays. That's the ABC Football Game of the Week. It's never over until midnight."

"You prefer watching football to making love?" Dr. Belladonna asked.

"That's a stupid question," the husband said angrily, "doesn't everybody?"

"Not *everybody*," Dr. Belladonna said. "Don't you find it strange that you prefer Howard Cosell to your own wife?"

"Are you trying to say I have homosexual tendencies?" the husband yelled.

"I didn't say that at all," Dr. Belladonna replied. "But it is true you'd rather watch twenty-two men knock each other down for three hours than make love to your wife."

"You're twisting things around," the husband said. "I can make love to my wife any time, but how often can I see a good football game?"

"All right, let's forget about Mondays," Dr. Belladonna said. "What about Tuesday night?"

"There's a basketball game to watch on Tuesday night. You want me to give up basketball, too?"

"I don't want you to give up anything. What about Wednesday nights?"

"He has hockey on Wednesday nights," the wife said.

"And Thursdays? Do you have anything to watch on Thursday nights?" Dr. Belladonna asked.

"No," said the husband. "But I'm pretty tired from staying up late on Monday, Tuesday, and Wednesday nights. A guy has to rest *sometime*."

"Fridays?" Dr. Belladonna asked.

"Friday is another basketball night," the husband said. "And Saturday night I like to get to bed early so I can watch the TV football games on Sunday afternoon."

"Well," said Dr. Belladonna, "that seems to take care of the week."

"Can you help us, Doctor?" the wife asked.

"It means a lot to us," the husband said. "We're willing to do anything to find happiness together."

Dr. Belladonna asked, "What are you doing for the rest of the afternoon?"

The husband looked at his TV guide, "This afternoon's no good. I have a golf game to watch at four." [7]

It is typical that when most men consult a physician, they expect that a physical cause will be readily found to explain their difficulty. If no physical cause is forthcoming, they may then begin to avoid sex by claiming that they are either too busy, too tired, or preoccupied with other matters. On the other hand, some men complain that they derive little pleasure or sensation from an orgasm. As far as sex is concerned, they feel they can either take it or leave it. Since it does not offer a particularly pleasurable sensation, they don't initiate sexual activity with their partner. In short, they just don't seem to be stimulated. The lack of a pleasurable sensation during emission and ejaculation is rarely caused by any organic disease; it is more often a reflection of a generalized disinterest in the sexual relationship. Underlying this complaint is usually one of the common emotions that cause impotence, such as anger, fear, boredom, or depression.

The breakdown of the sexual relationship between the male and the female has ramifications in their daily lives. Marital disputes are more common, and the husband and wife may end up criticizing each other over petty issues and fighting at the drop of a hat. All of this is simply evidence of frustration over sexual failure.

It must be emphasized that many, if not all, men at some time in their lives will become impotent, and that this involves many psychological causes. When the psychological problem is properly treated, normal sexual functioning often results. Chapter XI deals with treatment for the impotent man.

CHAPTER VII

PHYSICAL CAUSES OF IMPOTENCE

As previously stated, the causes of impotence are characteristically divided into two broad categories: psychological and physical. In general terms, the latter category refers to the inability to achieve an erection because of a physiological problem. This may be caused by an anatomic abnormality, a metabolic disorder, diseases of the nervous system, many systemic illnesses, surgical procedures such as the removal of a segment of the lower rectum, or a decrease in blood flow to the pelvis and penis that is associated with very advanced arteriosclerotic vascular disease. Some physical causes such as diabetes, alcohol, multiple sclerosis, paralysis, and impotence due to certain medications are common enough to warrant discussion in some detail. Some physical conditions preventing an erection may be present in the male from birth, others develop as a man grows older, and a few are actually self-inflicted. Some of the problems are readily treatable; others cannot be helped.

Unusual Causes

> *Though it be disfigured by many defects, to whom is his own body not dear?*
> —Franklin Edgerton

A very few unfortunate males are simply born without a penis. Although attempts have been made to construct one, the finished product is generally not ideal. Even if an organ whose appearance is satisfactory can be produced, it has no erectile ability. Another unusual physical deformity that may be associated with sexual dysfunction is a penis that is so small and hidden away in the scrotal skin that it can't be seen. Yet a third condition, in which the man has two penises, is known as diphallus. This is particularly rare and occurs in the United States once in approximately every five and a half million births.

Although many men are preoccupied with the thought that their penis is too small to permit them to function sexually, very few really have such a small phallus. However, some males do, in fact, have such a short organ that even in its erect state it is insufficient to permit penetration of the vagina. Such a small penis, known medically as a micropenis, usually results from a deficiency of stimulation of the organ by the male hormone testosterone. This is generally caused by a disorder of either the testicles, which produce this hormone, or the pituitary gland in the brain, which stimulates the testicles to produce the necessary hormone. If this condition does occur, it is often possible to promote penile growth by the administration of testosterone. However, it should be emphasized that this hormone should not be used by an individual who has a normal penis, and it should be used only in the treatment of testosterone deficiency.

A penis of sufficient length may be so deformed that it cannot be adequately inserted into the vagina. Some men are born with a condition called chordee, which causes the penis to bend downward in an arc. This is often associated with an abnormality in the location of the urethral opening, through which urine and semèn pass. Fortunately this can be surgically corrected. In men who have a condition called epispadias, the penis arcs upward and is usually associated with a short shaft. In addition, the urethra is not completely closed. The surgery required for this lesion is much more complicated and often less successful than that for chordee.

In another congenital disorder of the penis that may impede sexual intercourse, the penis deviates markedly to one side when it is erect. This anomaly occurs because one of the two erectile cylinders within the penis is longer than the other. Normally, they are essentially of equal length. Surgical correction involves shortening the longer cylinder, since there is no adequate means of lengthening the shorter one.

Males who have these last three conditions are born with them. However, there is one fairly common deformity of the penis that is not present at birth and that may be very disabling. Peyronie's disease refers to a condition in which there is dense scar tissue, usually located along the top of the penis and attached to the erectile cylinders. Why this scar tissue develops is not known. This illness is named after François de la Peyronie, the physician who first described the disease in 1743. Curiously, when the penis is soft it appears normal; however, if one feels along the top of the phallus, there is a firm area; this is where the scar is located. This scar causes the erect penis to angulate severely. This may cause great pain to the male and may also cause discomfort to the female since, in effect, during intercourse a curved object, rather than a straight one, is being thrust into the vagina. Naturally, the curved penis does not glide but is forced into the vagina. Peyronie's disease may improve by itself in time. However, if it does not, a multitude of treatments are available, including medication, surgical removal of the scar, steroid injections into the scar, or treatment with radiation. Unfortunately, none of these methods of treatment is always successful.

Another physical cause of impotence is trauma, in which either the penis or the testicles have been so severely injured that erection is not possible. The most drastic trauma that can befall the penis is amputation, either intentional or unintentional. Most intentional amputations are performed by surgeons in order to remove a cancer of the penis. However, one male came into a hospital emergency room bleeding profusely from the stump of his penis, which had been severed two hours earlier. In his right hand he was carrying a paper cup that contained the missing three and a half inches of his penis. His wife, whom he had married while he was in the army in Vietnam, had literally taken matters into her own hands when she discovered that he had been unfaithful to her. While he was asleep on the couch, she used a kitchen knife to get her revenge. In the operating room, the penis was reconnected, but the blood supply was sufficient to permit only a portion of the penis to survive and erections could not be achieved. However, surgical advances have been made in this area. In a very recent case, an angry husband avenged himself on his wife's boyfriend by taking a butcher knife and amputating the lover's penis. Physicians preserved the severed organ in a cool solution similar to that used for the preservation of kidneys prior to transplantation. Using microsurgical techniques, the appropriate arteries and veins were reconnected and the amputated penis was rejoined to its stump. The penis not only survived, but the patient is even able to achieve an erection. There are other patients who have had their penises successfully attached following amputation. Many of these do have erectile function, though most note a decrease in sensation. However, this does not seem to be an impediment to sexual gratification.

Surprising as it may seem, there are documented cases of men who have intentionally cut off their own penis or testicles, or both. Approximately fifty cases have been reported in the medical literature since 1900.[1,2] The cases are of bizarre interest. They include a twenty-five-year-old white man, a known paranoid schizophrenic, who removed his testicles and unsuccessfully attempted to amputate his penis with a razor blade. He had auditory hallucinations in which he heard his mother's voice directing him to carry out self-castration and penile amputation lest he be denied entry into the Kingdom of Heaven. An attempt to graft the testicles back to the body was unsuccessful. A thirty-year-old single white male college graduate, an engineer, amputated his penis at its base with a razor blade. The penis was brought to the hospital wrapped in a handkerchief by the patient himself. Surgical repair was attempted but was only partially successful. A forty-six-year-old unmarried white male physician, a pathologist, methodically placed his penis and testicles on a carving board in his kitchen and partially amputated the genitalia. Total removal was not accomplished because of the intense pain he experienced. This patient suffered from alcoholism and severe depression, both of which resulted from the discovery that he had cancer of the mouth. The surgical repair was partially successful, but one week later the patient committed suicide. One of the most unusual cases was that of a fifty-three-year-old white male pipe fitter who performed self-emasculation and cannibalism. He cut off his penis, scrotum, and testicles and swallowed them. Amazingly, after psychotherapy he was able to return to his usual employment. A forty-nine-year-old married machinist with two children was brought to the hospital by his wife, who was carrying a small paper bag containing both of her husband's testicles, which he had earlier removed while under the influence of alcohol. After the patient had undergone four months of psychiatric therapy, artificial testicles were placed in his scrotum. These testicles are not functional and serve only a cosmetic purpose.

A review of the cases involving self-mutilation reveals many common themes. The patient is usually either an only child or the youngest in the family. His mother is very demanding and dominant; she expects complete obedience from her child. When the child misbehaves, she usually responds with physical abuse. She prefers that her son be passive. Many of the mothers themselves are schizophrenic. The fathers of these patients are often away from home for prolonged periods of time. Many eventually divorce their wives. Those fathers who do stay at home are very shy and reticent. In some cases the patient grew up without a father.

Some physicians have hypothesized that the self-mutilating male is seeking the ultimate identification with his mother. At any rate, all of these patients are obviously severely mentally disturbed.

Most injuries to the penis are not intentional. Nor are they as severe as in the above-mentioned cases. Usually the penis is simply lacerated or bruised. Most accidental injuries occur when the penis is in its erect state. The soft, or flaccid, penis usually hangs out of the way.

One particularly serious injury that may occur when the penis is erect is a fracture. Unlike the whale and the walrus, man does not have a bone within his penis, but the cylindrical erectile bodies within it may actually tear with trauma. Vigorous coitus may cause such a fracture. One unfortunate gentleman was just about to engage in intercourse and had a firm erection. He arose from his bed to close the window, as the breeze was chilly. Because the window was stuck, he raised his arms and pulled down with all his strength, failing to realize that his penis protruded across the sill. As the window slammed shut, he became very much aware of this, and shortly thereafter was driven to the hospital.

Another case of a fractured penis involved a forty-eight-year-old welder who came to the emergency room with a severely swollen penis. At its largest point it was eight inches in circumference and was bent acutely at a ninety-degree angle. The patient related the following story to the physician. He had achieved an erection during foreplay with his wife and was attempting to insert his penis into her vagina. He misdirected the penis so that it hit his wife's pelvic bone. He felt his penis snap and believed that he heard it cracking as well. Swelling immediately occurred. The pain was not excessive, but he realized that he was in need of help and came to the hospital. The patient was taken to the operating room, where a fracture of the erectile cylinders was repaired.

A fracture of the penis may be sewn shut and successful erections may occur again, though this is not always the case. Frequently the penis will be severely angulated when erect, and further surgery may have to be performed in order to straighten it.

Another physical cause of impotence that may be transient is trauma to the area between the legs just behind the male scrotum. The usual cause is a straddle injury in which the male receives a blow from an object or during a fall. The following case history is illustrative.

J. M., a twenty-four-year-old male, went to his doctor complaining of inability to achieve an erection. Seven weeks before, he had sustained an injury in the following manner. While relaxing near a riverbank, he saw a canoe overturn in the water. Dashing toward the river to help, he leaped over a small iron object in his path. He did not completely clear the metal structure and received a hard blow between the rectum and the scrotum. He had no difficulty with urination after the incident, but was unable to have an erection. He had never had any problem with sexual function before. The doctor's physical examination showed that the man was entirely normal. Six weeks later, he was seen in follow-up and his erectile ability was already markedly improved. He was now able to penetrate, although the penis was not as rigid as usual. Three months later, he was functioning in an entirely normal fashion.

This kind of injury causes a temporary lack of erectile ability. However, in some cases, men report that they have never been able to function successfully again.

Another physical cause of impotence is pain. Some males complain of pain in the penis before and during intercourse. In some men, the pain seems to be imaginary, since no physical cause can be found. However, in other individuals, examination reveals inflammation or irritation of either the head or the foreskin of the penis. One of the most renowned cases of impotence was that of Louis XVI of France, who reigned from 1774 to 1793. At age sixteen he married Marie Antoinette, who was then only fifteen. For the first seven years of his marriage, the king could not have an erection. Eventually his physicians determined that the cause of the king's impotence was pain caused by a tight foreskin. He was circumcised and thereafter was able to perform successfully.

Various portions of the male genital system have been implicated in the failure to achieve an erection. The prostate is mentioned more often than any other genital organ. However, it is more probable that individuals who have a chronic low-grade inflammation of the prostate are impotent because of psychological reasons and simply use their physical illness as a rationalization. A typical example, and one that is often seen by urologists, is the man who has contracted an inflammation of the prostate sometime after having begun an extramarital affair. These individuals have such a guilty conscience that impotence develops. They are thoroughly convinced that their problem is the inflammation, but in fact this is rarely the case. Unfortunately, many doctors have reinforced the notion that illnesses such as chronic prostatitis are responsible for impotence. Some physicians actually believe this, but it provides others with a ready explanation for the patient and avoids involvement in the psychological aspects of the case. Consideration of a patient's problems is time-consuming, and besides, few patients want to hear that their problem is in their head.

Other causes of impotence are painful ejaculation and blood in the semen. If ejaculation is a painful experience, a male may wish to avoid having erections altogether. This is similar to the young child with a urinary infection who avoids emptying his bladder because it hurts. Pain on ejaculation is usually caused by inflammation or infection of the prostate gland, and it may occur at any age. If the reproductive glands become inflamed or infected, a male may note that blood is present in the semen and become frightened. This condition, called hematospermia, usually responds to antibiotics in conjunction with a short course of the female hormone diethylstilbestrol.

A massive enlargement of the scrotum may interfere with intercourse and make it difficult to maintain an erection. A hydrocele refers to an unusually large accumulation of fluid within the sac that normally surrounds the testicle. It may occur on either side or on both sides simultaneously. There are usually no significant symptoms other than enlargement, although a dragging sensation is sometimes described by a patient. Occasionally the scrotum becomes so large that the penis seems to retract and is partially hidden. Fortunately this condition can be treated by a surgical procedure in which the fluid is drained.

The Leriche sydrome refers to a medical condition in which there is very advanced atherosclerosis, which causes a blockage of blood flow through the major blood vessels of the pelvis. This condition was first described in 1922, and clinically is characterized by a patient's complaint that he tires easily or suffers from pain in his legs. The leg discomfort may be present in either one or both extremities and may involve either the thigh, calf, or foot. Patients suffering from this disease may be impotent. This condition can frequently be treated by placement of a vascular graft, which restores blood flow to the pelvis and penis. Evidence also suggests that atherosclerosis may affect smaller blood vessels, but unfortunately these are not so readily treated.

A relatively recent cause of impotence is exposure to external voltage radiation. X-ray treatment is now a popular form of therapy for certain cancers. Malignancies frequently treated in this way are cancers of the bowel, prostate, and bladder. While physicians have known for some time of potential adverse side effects of radiation therapy, they have only recently become aware that impotence may occur. Among patients treated with radiation for prostatic cancer, at least 30 percent, and in some studies 80 percent, have been unable to achieve an erection sufficient to permit vaginal penetration. It is uncertain whether this loss of erectile function will be permanent, but some individuals are still unable to function many years after completing their treatment. To most men, however, the benefits of this treatment outweigh its disadvantages. It must be emphasized that the radiation dose commonly used in diagnostic X-ray studies, such as those for the bowel and kidneys, does not cause impotence.

Many of the examples I have cited here are unusual and do not account for a significant number of cases of impotence. Some are rare enough to be considered medical curiosities.

More common physical causes of impotence are alcohol, certain medications, and diabetes. These deserve special emphasis.

What Effects Does Alcohol Have on Erections?

Lechery Sir, it provokes and unprovokes; it provokes the desire but takes away performance.

—Shakespeare, *Macbeth*

The above comment about alcohol, made by the porter in *Macbeth* (act 2, scene 3), clearly tells us what effect alcohol has upon erections. That alcohol is an impediment to erections often comes as a surprise to many men. Some males rely upon alcohol to loosen them up and make them more outgoing. Then, to their disappointment, they find they cannot perform the sex act.

Alcohol may, in fact, be the most common worldwide cause of secondary impotence. It is not generally known and understood that alcohol is a depressant and not a stimulant. The chronic use of alcohol may exert adverse effects by causing nerve damage, liver failure through cirrhosis, and a generalized state of malnutrition. In addition, the testicles may shrink and cease to function properly. As one alcoholic said, "I started out like Early Times but ended up like Old Grandad."

R. F., a twenty-two-year-old college senior, complained to his doctor that he had been unable to achieve an erection the previous Saturday night. He had always been a "bedroom athlete" and prided himself on being able to have intercourse with his date three or four times a night. On this occasion, he had ingested a significant quantity of alcohol; following his overindulgence he could not achieve an erection despite his partner's manual and oral stimulation of his penis. This caused him great embarrassment and raised in his mind the question of whether he was a normal male. After being counseled to limit his alcoholic intake prior to future sexual marathons, R. F. later reported no further difficulties with impotence.

M. M., a forty-seven-year-old corporate vice-president, attended a company banquet in honor of his boss. He rarely abused alcohol, but on this occasion he had several strong drinks after dinner. He became rather loud, and once even fell on the dance floor, much to his wife's embarrassment. When she urged him to control himself and cease drinking, he responded with some harsh words, which set a cool tone for the rest of the evening. Finally M. M.'s wife drove him home. Feeling rather amorous, he attempted to undress his wife, but she pulled away. In bed, his advances were rejected until he became rather forceful. Though his wife was in no mood for intercourse, she decided the best thing to do would be to cooperate and get the whole matter over with. Assuming the superior position, M. M. attempted to penetrate his wife but was surprised to find that his penis was limp. After several clumsy motions he gave up, and he and his wife fell asleep.

M. M.'s sexual encounters over the next several months were successful. However, he gradually began to increase his drinking until he found he could not relax unless he had three cocktails before dinner, and he generally had another drink before retiring. Because of increased business pressures, he began to have one or two martinis almost daily during business lunches. He began arriving late for work and failed to meet many of his deadlines. Despite warnings about his poor performance, he continued to drink and eventually was fired. By this time, his wife was threatening divorce and pleading with him to seek professional help, which he refused to do.

When she moved out of the house, his drinking increased. Finally a friend persuaded him to attend a meeting of Alcoholics Anonymous, but he went only once. He continued to drink, and would go on binges that lasted for several days. He was hospitalized for acute gastrointestinal bleeding secondary to alcoholic gastritis. He stopped drinking, but for only two weeks. After a while, he was able to acquire a low-level bureaucratic job, where his performance was spotty.

Over the ensuing years he became somewhat of a loner. He suffered from cirrhosis of the liver and showed other signs of chronic alcohol abuse, such as diminished testicle size and a ruddy facial complexion. On several occasions he attempted intercourse with women he met in bars but was unable to attain an erection.

He was hospitalized on several occasions for pneumonia and a generally debilitated state of health. Each hospitalization was complicated by an abrupt withdrawal from alcohol, and he would suffer delirium tremens. Despite repeated suggestions that he go for psychiatric counseling, he refused all help. He remains a chronic alcoholic. He is totally impotent.

Alcohol should not be ingested in significant quantities if a male is having difficulty achieving erections. However, in limited amounts it is not harmful. No precise guidelines can be provided as to the quantities of alcohol one can ingest because, like sex, what is too much for one man isn't enough for another. Unfortunately, as a man becomes intoxicated, there are no warning signals to tell him that he has reached a point at which he will be unable to perform sexually.

Is the Cause of Your Impotence in Your Medicine Cabinet?

Leave the life there at its ease, let it take care of itself, it will do better than if you paralyze it by loading it with medicine.

—Napoleon

There is a great deal of drug use in our society. Yet some of our most important and commonly used drugs can have adverse side effects, including impotence. Some of these medicines either delay or stop ejaculation altogether.[3,4] Others cause a decrease in libido.

Many of the medicines that if taken improperly can cause sexual dysfunction are prescribed for high blood pressure. Since there are approximately twenty-three million patients in the United States who have this illness, the sex lives of a great many men may suffer.

The following drugs have been known to cause sexual difficulties in some men. They are listed by their non-proprietary name; trade names, where given, appear in parentheses.

antispasmodies	atropine
	diphenhydramine
	propantheline (Pro-Banthine)
sedatives	barbiturates
	alcohol
	flurazepam
high blood pressure medications	chlorothiazide
	guanethidine (Ismelin)
	hydralazine
	methyldopa (Aldomet)
	clonidine (Catapres)
	spironolactone (Aldactone, Aldactazide)
	reserpine
antianxiety agents	meprobamate
	diazepam (Valium)

	chlordiazepoxide
	oxazepam (Serax)
narcotics	codeine
	meperidine
	oxycodone
	heroin
antidepressants	tricyclics (Tofranil, Elavil, Pertofrane)
	MAO inhibitors (Parnate, Marplan, Nardil)
stimulants	epinephrine
	amphetamines (Benzedrine)
	caffeine
	ephedrine
major tranquilizers	phenothiazines (Mellaril, Prolixin)
	haloperidol (Haldol)
estrogens	diethylstilbestrol (Stilbestrol)
	chlorotrianisene (TACE)

If a man is impotent or having another difficulty in his sexual functioning, then it is important that he consult with his physician concerning the type and quantity of his medication. No patient should discontinue medication that may be causing impotence without first obtaining his physician's advice, especially since most of the medications listed don't cause any difficulty if the proper dosage is taken.

Can Diabetes Affect the Male Sexual Function?

Life is not a spectacle or a feast; it is a predicament.

—George Santayana

The incidence of diabetes is rising by almost 6 percent a year in the United States. It is predicted that the number of people affected will double in the next fifteen years, reaching a total figure of approximately twenty million. Surveys indicate that at least five million persons know or suspect that they have diabetes and that another five million are undiagnosed.

It is estimated that nearly 50 percent of male diabetics will become impotent, but it is not possible to predict which ones will suffer from impotence since there is no correlation between impotence and the duration of the diabetes or the degree of control that has been achieved over the disease.

Impotence may, in fact, be the first sign of the onset of diabetes mellitus and in any male who is having difficulty achieving erections, this possibility must be considered. Another infrequently recognized sign of the onset of diabetes is phimosis. In this condition an un-circumcised male finds that he can no longer retract the foreskin. When this occurs in middle adult life, the patient will prove to be diabetic one-third of the time.

Diabetes may affect the male's sexual functioning in a multitude of ways. He may find that he is unable to perform sexually at all, or he may, in fact, be able to ejaculate after appropriate stimulation, but never achieve an erection. Or he may be able to achieve a normal erection and have an orgasm, but no semen will be forthcoming from the penis. This is because the ejaculation occurs in a retrograde fashion and enters the bladder. It is washed out at the time that the patient voids. In the diabetic male, the sex drive is usually normal. Here is a typical history of an impotent diabetic:

F. T., a forty-two-year-old male, complained of difficulty in achieving a firm erection. He noted that he had to "stuff" the penis into his partner's vagina because it would not become stiff enough to permit penetration. He could have intercourse in this fashion, and it did culminate in an ejaculation and orgasm, but it wasn't satisfying to him or to his female partner. He could masturbate with a soft penis and ejaculate. He never awakened with an erection.

Until recently, the diabetic male who was totally impotent as a result of his disease could be offered little more than sympathy, of which he frequently got little. This was a sad fate for many men who were only in their thirties and forties. But now the picture is brighter. The management of the diabetic with sexual disorders includes establishing good control of the diabetic state. This may correct the early attacks of impotence. Unfortunately, as the disease continues, impotence usually becomes permanent and is not reversible. The impotent diabetic male and his spouse may well profit from sexual counseling. An explanation of what is occurring keeps unrealistic demands from being imposed upon the male. Male hormones have not proved to be of value in treating this illness, and may only aggravate the patient's psychological difficulties by increasing his sex drive but in no way helping his performance. Fortunately, it is now possible to implant a prosthesis into the penis that will permit the male to achieve penetration of the vagina. Prostheses are discussed in a later chapter in a section on the surgical treatment of impotence.

There are several other medical conditions, including priapism, multiple sclerosis, stroke, and paralysis, that may cause impotence.

Priapism

> *If a man could have half his wishes, he would double his troubles.*
>
> —Benjamin Franklin

Priapism refers to a persistent erection that may occur without any sexual stimulation and that persists long beyond sexual desire. It is not unusual during an attack of priapism to have a continuous erection for two to three days at a time. The condition was named after Priapus, the ancient Greek god of fertility. Pictures of Priapus portray him as the proud possessor of a huge, distended phallus.

D. W. M. is a thirty-six-year-old male with a history of normal sexual functioning. Having taken off an entire day from work to be with his girl friend, he had successful coitus with her early in the morning. Coitus was repeated without difficulty approximately one hour later. However, at this time he noted that following ejaculation and orgasm the penis did not return to its normal soft state. His initial reaction was pride and satisfaction, and hence only half an hour elapsed before he again penetrated his female partner. Following withdrawal of the penis, he noted that it still maintained its rigid state. Six hours elapsed, and the penis had not lost any of its firmness; the sexual act was repeated. That evening, approximately twelve hours after his initial erection, his feelings of pride and wonder had shifted to concern. Within a few hours, pain in the penis had begun to develop and he again had intercourse, hoping that one more ejaculation would return his penis to its normal soft state. This did not occur, and several hours later he came to the emergency room.

He was sedated with narcotics, but still the penis stood upright. By this time it was throbbing and painful. The narcotics were continued, but only to relieve his pain. He was taken to the operating room, where large needles were passed into the shaft of the penis, and the blood, which had become thick and sludgelike, was sucked out. However, within fifteen minutes the penis was again erect, and an incision was made beneath the scrotum so that the blood could be drained from the erectile tissue. Following this, a vein was sewn into the erectile tissue so that it could carry away the blood that continued to swell the penis.

The operation was successful, and the penis remained in a limp state. But three months after the operation, D. W. M. could achieve only a partial erection, which was not firm enough to penetrate his female partner.

The medical diagnosis for this condition is priapism. Men who develop it are usually pleased at first, particularly if its onset coincides with sexual activity. Their female partners are usually equally pleased. However, as hours pass and the erection persists, pain develops, and what was once a source of delight has become a source of concern. The cause of the condition is generally never determined, although many illnesses are known to play a role in priapism, including certain blood diseases such as sickle-cell disease and leukemia. Carbon monoxide or carbon dioxide poisoning have also been mentioned as possible factors.

There is no one agreed-upon treatment for priapism. Some physicians recommend that the patient be anesthetized in hopes that the penis will be decompressed. Others have recommended ice water enemas. Most treatment today consists of one or another of several surgical procedures that are designed to allow the blood causing the erection to drain from the penis.

Of great concern is the fact that a single episode of this condition may leave the patient totally impotent, since the erectile tissue becomes scarred from the persistent erection.

Fortunately, this condition is not common. A practicing urologist may see one or two such cases in his lifetime.

Multiple sclerosis, stroke, and paralysis affect a significant portion of our society, yet few people are aware of the effect these conditions have upon sexual functioning.

Multiple Sclerosis

Multiple sclerosis is not an uncommon disease. It is characterized by impairment of the nervous system in many different areas of the body. A patient may have an acute attack whose symptoms may later seem to disappear, but after several such episodes, the nervous system is permanently injured. Many different parts of the body are of course affected, and sexual functioning is not spared. Initially the sexual disturbance may be temporary, but sometime in the future it becomes permanent.

In the male with multiple sclerosis, impotence is common. A man suffering from the disease may be able to get an erection, but it may not be sustained. Some men's ejaculations are uncontrollable, while others find that they cannot ejaculate at all. The penis may fail to become hard and therefore be too limp to achieve penetration.

In addition, sensation may be impaired. The male may relate that he cannot feel whether his penis is in the vagina. Some men describe a numbness in their testicles.

Because multiple sclerosis is potentially so crippling, it engenders a great deal of anxiety, fear, and depression in those affected. These emotions in themselves may cause the male to be secondarily impotent. In these cases, sexual counseling may be of value. Unfortunately, at this time there is no cure for the disease itself.

Stroke

Cerebrovascular accidents, commonly known as strokes, are among the most frequent cripplers today. Most men who suffer this catastrophe are initially seriously ill, and many do not survive. Those who do may be left with serious physiological and psychological impairments. A male may be paralyzed in an arm or a leg, for instance, or he may be unable to speak. He may be confronted with the necessity of having to use a cane or a wheelchair for the rest of his life. He may have a multitude of worries, including whether his family and friends will accept him, whether he will lose his job, or how he will support his family. On top of this mountain of concerns is another very important one: sexual functioning. Most stroke patients do not lose their libido, and so concern over whether they will be able to perform sexually becomes paramount. And naturally the female partner of the stroke victim wonders at some point whether she will ever again enjoy the pleasure of sexual intercourse.

In most cases, unless the brain damage has been very extensive, an erection can be attained and successful intercourse completed. However, studies indicate that the frequency of intercourse often declines after a stroke.

Paralysis

Many people have wondered whether a friend or acquaintance or someone they pass on the street who is paralyzed can ever have sexual intercourse. The answer is that many can, and there is no doubt that sex is very important to these individuals.

In general, injuries to the upper spine cause more sexual difficulties than those involving the lower spine. If a person has an injury in which the upper portion of his spinal cord is involved, it is quite likely that he can have erections that are brought on by stimulation of the penis. However, these individuals can generally not achieve an erection by such common means as viewing pornographic material or thinking erotic thoughts. About 70 percent of these individuals who attempt intercourse will be successful, though they cannot ejaculate and will not experience an orgasm, and certainly will not be able to create a pregnancy.

Of those patients whose lower portion of the spinal cord is injured, about 25 percent will be able to have erections that can be brought about by viewing stimulating material or having stimulating sexual thoughts. Of this 25 percent, approximately 65 percent can have successful coitus, and nearly 20 percent can ejaculate and have an orgasm. Approximately 5 percent can sire children.[5]

Fertility is reduced in males who are paralyzed. This is due not only to the sexual dysfunction that has occurred following an injury to the nervous system, but also to the fact that the testicles do not produce sperm efficiently. This is most likely due to the loss of temperature regulation involving the testicles. Normally the testicles are maintained at a temperature of 2.2° C. less than body temperature. This is why males normally note that during a hot shower or bath their testicles seem to hang lower than normal, and when they enter a cold swimming pool their testicles draw upward into the body. In paralysis this control is lost, along with the delicate regulation of blood flow to the testicles, which is necessary for normal sperm production.

Generally speaking, sexual function among spinal-cord-injury patients declines at an earlier age than among men who do not have such an injury. A case study of a young paralyzed male poignantly illustrates this problem.

The patient, age twenty-three, was injured three years prior when he was struck in the back by a bullet fired by a policeman, injuring the upper portion of the spinal cord. This tragedy was compounded by the fact that there was an apparent case of mistaken identity and the patient was, in fact, not a criminal. Despite this, he amazingly retained a healthy attitude toward the outside world and showed few signs of self-pity.

Commenting upon the function of his penis he noted: "Well, the biggest thing, you don't control it no more. It controls itself. At times you may be sitting down and playing cards or something, and you won't have women or sex on your mind and all of a sudden it rises. And then, at times that you want it, it won't respond."

He was able to engage in intercourse if his wife manually stimulated the penis, but he was not able to ejaculate or have an orgasm. During intercourse, his wife was able to climax and he described his feelings: "All the time you're figuring what you could do if you could still have the movements of your hips and discharge, instead of feeling nothing happens. You may get a warm sensation but like I said, most of the feelings are in your head." He noted that kissing "makes you feel a whole lot better than it would for a woman to try to have intercourse with you . . . because you can feel it when somebody kisses you with feelings in it. . . ."

Summing up his feelings he related that "it's altogether different than it was before I got hurt. It's gone away from you, it's just gone. There's nothing you can do about that. They say it's twice a child, and once a man. Well, you were a man for a while, so now you just go on back to a child." [6]

Dr. Theodore Cole has offered a description that is designed to facilitate our understanding of the disability a paralyzed person faces.

It would be helpful if the reader would imagine that he has become suddenly paraplegic. He is totally paralyzed and has lost all ability to feel bodily sensations from the mid chest down. He is a head and shoulders floating in space. He can still feel normally above the mid-chest area. Automatic bodily functions have been altered and bladder and bowel control has been lost. The bladder may empty itself spontaneously into diapers or clothing, or it may be continually drained off by a tube in the bladder which passes out of the urethra and travels down to a plastic bag strapped to the leg and filled full of urine. Because bowel control has also been lost, fecal incontinence can occur at any time. There is no superficial or deep sensation in the genitals, and one would have to be watching to know that the genitals were being touched or manipulated. The physical experience of orgasm no longer can occur. In the case of the male, erotic stimulation which previously produced erections no longer does. The body has become abruptly altered and its normal contours have been changed. Areas of looseness and sagging may appear together with other areas of atrophy and loss of muscle mass. The individual can no longer stand or walk. He moves about seated in a wheelchair, causing him to converse with erect people by looking upward. Everyone is taller than he. It is not difficult to imagine that this altered body condition could lead to self-consciousness and feelings of inadequacy which may cause the individual to actively avoid sexual encounter. Yet through all this it must be remembered that the capacity for psychosexual enjoyment remains in most people thus disabled.[7]

CHAPTER VIII
OTHER SEXUAL CRISES

There are other sexual crises that may affect a male besides the inability to achieve an erection. These are uncontrollable ejaculation, the inability to ejaculate, non-ejaculatory intercourse, and declining orgasmic intensity. These are significant problems by themselves, but in addition, each may cause impotence.

Uncontrollable Ejaculation

> *A man of sense may be in haste, but can never be in a hurry.*
>
> —Lord Chesterfield

Uncontrollable or premature ejaculation is a very common problem. As many as 30 percent of cases of impotence may be preceded by this condition, and thus it may be the most common factor associated with impotence. If a male cannot sustain an erection long enough for his female partner to achieve an orgasm, he may feel that he is not really meeting his sexual responsibility. And if his female partner tells him that he is not satisfying her, he may become impotent. For as the male appears to be concentrating, and tries harder and harder to achieve an erection and maintain it for a longer period of time, he is actually distracting himself, so much so that eventually he finds that he cannot achieve an erection at all.

The typical history of this type of impotence is of a male who ejaculates following minimal sexual stimulation. This generally occurs with all of his partners, and as a result of his embarrassment at having failed to satisfy his partner, he becomes preoccupied with trying to prolong his erection prior to ejaculation. During intercourse, he may actually count to himself or otherwise try to distract himself mentally. He may reduce his thrusting activity but, despite his best efforts, will ejaculate before, during, or just after vaginal penetration. Most of the time, his partner will not have time to reach her climax.

To define premature ejaculation is not easy. Kinsey noted that 75 percent of males ejaculate within two minutes of penetration. Ejaculation in less than this time could be considered premature. Others have suggested that ejaculation prior to ten active thrusts constitutes this condition. Masters and Johnson have defined premature ejaculation as occurring when a man cannot sustain his erection long enough for his partner to have an orgasm prior to his ejaculation at least 50 percent of the time. This definition is not applicable if the female is unable to achieve orgasm for reasons other than the male's rapid ejaculation. It is generally accepted that Kinsey's definition, which was formulated more than twenty-five years ago, is not applicable to today's society. Men are currently more conscious of the female's feelings during intercourse and feel more compelled to ensure that she has an orgasm. For this reason, it is more likely that intercourse lasts closer to between two and five minutes before ejaculation, but this is at best an estimate. And no one is really certain how long the sex act should last. Some men feel that they are very accomplished lovers if they can pull off a "quickie," while others feel they demonstrate their masculinity by prolonging intercourse.

Wide variation exists not only among humans but also in the animal kingdom. On the one hand, chimpanzees may complete the act in sixteen seconds, while mink may remain in the coital position for as long as eight hours. Different cultures also display this kind of variability. Men among the Ifugao of the Philippines ejaculate almost immediately upon insertion of the penis into the vagina, while the Hopi Indians attempt to delay ejaculation for as long as possible.[1]

Perhaps the earliest recorded case of premature ejaculation is found in Greek mythology. Erichthonius, a mythical king of Athens, was conceived when Hephaestus, the Greek god of fire, ejaculated upon Gaea, goddess of the earth. This story was mentioned by Euripides and was recorded elsewhere in the following passage:

Athena came to Hephaestus desirous to get arms. He, being forsaken by Aphrodite, fell in love with Athena and began to pursue her; but she fled. When he got near her with much ado (for he was lame), he attempted to embrace her: but she being a chaste virgin, would not submit to him, and he dropped his seed on the leg of the goddess. In disgust she wiped off the seed with wool and threw it on the ground and Erichtonius was produced.[2]

It simply isn't known how long the average male keeps his penis in the vagina before he ejaculates. It has been stated that men from lower socioeconomic groups believe that rapid ejaculation is a sign of increased masculinity. On the other end of the economic scale, it is generally felt that prolonging the sex act is desirable. More men in this group feel concern about helping the female achieve orgasm each time they have intercourse.

In reality, very little is achieved by trying to arrive at an average. It will only make some men who are actually well adjusted seem inadequate if they find that they fall below the average. And many of these men's wives may currently be thoroughly satisfied sexually.

Premature ejaculation may be more severe for certain men than for others. In most cases, the afflicted male ejaculates shortly after he penetrates the vagina. However, in extreme cases, a male may ejaculate simply at the sight of a female's nude body or as soon as he touches his female partner.

In most men, ejaculatory control increases with experience. Many teenagers, particularly in their early sexual encounters, have very little control, and may even ejaculate before they can get their zipper down.

The causes of uncontrollable ejaculation are manifold. As I have mentioned, physical illness, such as multiple sclerosis, may be a cause. Also, urologists used to ascribe uncontrollable ejaculation to inflammation of the prostate gland. However, it is recognized today that most cases are psychological in origin. If a spouse or other sexual partner has little interest in sex and admonishes her mate to "hurry up and get it over with fast," premature ejaculation may result. A husband who subconsciously wishes to punish his wife by denying her the pleasure of an orgasm may do so by ejaculating prematurely. Habit may be responsible, too. Those men whose primary sexual experience has been with prostitutes, and who have always hurried through the act, are a good example of this. Teenagers whose sexual activities usually occur in their date's home may develop this condition since they always feel rushed to finish before the girl's parents return. Lack of proper information on the part of the male may also be responsible. Some men do not understand that it takes females longer to become aroused sexually, and even longer to reach an orgasm.

Many males are uncertain whether their partners reach an orgasm, and unfortunately are too embarrassed to ask. Is there any way that a man can tell if his partner is really climaxing, and not pretending in order to preserve his ego? Some women are capable of imitating an orgasm by sensuous writhing and by moaning with apparent delight. Definite physical responses occur during the female orgasm. There is a sudden coolness of the lips and the face as the blood is drained away. This is associated with a facial expression that depicts agony rather than pleasure. The skin on the chest may appear flushed or red. Rhythmic muscular contractions of the body and vagina occur. Other less easily recognizable signs include increased prominence of the nipples and a change of color of the inner lips of the vagina.

After repeated acts of intercourse with the same partner, the male may be able to detect when the woman has been sexually satisfied. But if intercourse is occurring with a stranger or with someone who is seen infrequently, a man probably cannot be certain if his partner has climaxed.

If a man has a truly close relationship with his female partner and is concerned about whether or not she is sexually satisfied, he should simply ask her.

Inability to Ejaculate

A very significant problem, albeit less common than uncontrollable ejaculation, is the inability to ejaculate during intercourse. A full erection occurs but semen is not forthcoming, nor is an orgasm experienced. Active thrusting during intercourse is prolonged, and either the male or female or both may become physically exhausted.

Jack and his wife were initially seen for an infertility evaluation. They had been married for one year and had had unprotected intercourse during that period of time. His wife had not undergone a gynecological examination, but her menstrual periods were regular. Physical examination revealed that Jack was an entirely normal male, and analysis showed his semen was of good quality.

After fifteen minutes of interviewing the couple jointly, the wife mentioned that intercourse "seemed to take so long." Careful questioning revealed that Jack achieved an erection without difficulty but that coitus persisted, often for as long as forty-five minutes. While the wife was capable of multiple orgasms, she complained of pelvic and back discomfort because of the prolonged thrusting.

Finally the doctor uncovered the fact that Jack was incapable of ejaculating when his penis was in the vagina. Jack admitted that this had been true in other sexual encounters he had had prior to his marriage. He usually culminated the sexual act by withdrawing the penis and masturbating by compressing his penis against the bed sheets.

The patient was referred for psychiatric counseling and remains in treatment.

Many theories have been offered as to why this condition develops, but none has been proved. Some psychiatrists feel it is a result of a male's desire to maintain a constant erection as a demonstration of his manhood. Others believe it is an unconscious attempt to punish the female partner by denying her the pleasure and satisfaction of knowing her partner has ejaculated. In some cases it may involve a male's fear of causing a pregnancy.

Some doctors have suggested that the inability to ejaculate when the penis is contained in the vagina is due to a man's overcontrolling his emotions.[3] This overcontrol is an attempt to decrease anxiety. Men who experience this kind of difficulty are usually not able to relax fully. They generally have obsessive-compulsive personalities, and many are noted to have difficulty in making decisions and spending money.

Why these individuals have such a high level of anxiety is unknown. It is hypothesized that it is because of earlier developmental experiences. Some psychiatrists have suggested that some of these individuals have had mothers who have been overprotective, while others may have had experiences with women who rejected them.

Regardless of the cause of the problem, the male becomes preoccupied with his ability to perform during his next sexual encounter. In addition, he is overly concerned with his partner's possible response. He worries that she may be angry if he can't perform.

When inability to ejaculate is a problem, it is easy to understand how the male and female become discouraged and may avoid sexual intercourse altogether. Some males eventually become impotent.

Fortunately, ejaculatory failure is uncommon. Most men who suffer from this condition do so sporadically and may ejaculate and have orgasm at times. For those men who never ejaculate or have an orgasm, psychiatric counseling is indicated in order to determine the emotional conflict that may be causing the problem, since it is rarely physical.

In addition to psychiatric therapy, sexual counseling using a form of behavior modification may be effective. The male must be desensitized so that he can ejaculate in the presence of his female partner. This is accomplished first by masturbation in which the male's only stimulation is erotic fantasies or pornographic literature, and finally by manual or oral stimulation by the female.

After an ejaculation has been achieved by both of these methods, the male is stimulated and then instructed to enter the vagina just as he is about to ejaculate. If his erection fades, manual or oral stimulation is again resumed until the male can eventually penetrate and have an intravaginal orgasm. This method requires great patience and is not always successful.

Nonejaculatory Intercourse

There is another category of nonejaculatory intercourse, in which a man is able to have an erection, penetrate, and have an orgasm, but semen does not spurt forth from the end of the penis. This is due to malfunction of the bladder neck—the opening to the bladder. Individuals with this problem do secrete semen into the penis, but because the bladder neck does not close, the semen travels backward (retrograde) into the bladder.

The first time the patient urinates, the semen is washed out of the bladder. Thus, these individuals do have an orgasm, and most notice no decrease in the pleasurable sensation associated with the sexual act and orgasm. The most common causes of retrograde ejaculation are prostate surgery in which the bladder neck is disrupted, diabetes, and spinal cord injury. Some medication, primarily that used for the treatment of high blood pressure, will also cause this problem. Discontinuation of the medicine will reverse the condition.

Declining Orgasmic Intensity

Some males complain that the quality of their orgasms has declined. These individuals note that the pleasurable sensation associated with ejaculation is not as great as it once was. In extreme cases, the semen is discharged either without the man's having any sensory awareness or with only minimal sensation. If this condition is severe enough, impotence can result.

This problem is generally not traceable to any physical cause, for the intensity of an orgasm is dependent upon psychological factors. These include such variables as the setting in which sexual activity is occurring, the feeling toward the female partner, the amount of foreplay, the female's physical response to stimulation, and the amount of time that has elapsed since the previous orgasm.

There is no specific treatment for this problem other than providing the male with these facts. Fortunately, this difficulty is usually short-lived. If a male understands why his orgasm varies in intensity from time to time, he should not become anxious. The situation will usually improve.

CHAPTER IX
MYTHS AND FALLACIES

The topic of sex is veiled in myths and fallacies. So is the subject of impotence. There are several factors that many men and women believe are responsible for impotence. These include heart attacks, masturbation, common operations, the length of the penis, penis captivus, and venereal disease. What are the facts?

Heart Attacks

> *"The trouble is, Sancho,"* said Don Quixote,
> *"you are so afraid that you cannot see or hear*
> *properly: for one of the effects of fear is to*
> *disturb the senses and cause things to appear*
> *other than what they are."*
>
> —Cervantes

The male patient recovering from a heart attack is placed in a dependent position, since he now must rely heavily upon his family and friends, and certainly upon his physician. This dependence may diminish his feelings of masculinity. If his doctor does not bring up the matter of his future sexual life, he may conclude that intercourse is beyond his physical capability. Masters and Johnson have noted that two-thirds of those patients who recovered from a heart attack received no sexual advice whatsoever from their physicians. And in many of those cases in which advice was rendered, it was vague and not clearly understood.

A male convalescing from a heart attack often has a decreased libido. In addition, he may fear that he will die during intercourse in the so-called "death in the saddle" manner. Many patients are hesitant to ask their physician's advice either out of embarrassment or for fear of being told that their sexual life is over. Similarly, many wives are concerned with the situation but are reluctant to inquire because they do not want to put pressure on their husbands. Some women feel intercourse may cause too great a strain on their husband's heart and may withhold themselves, thereby making the male increasingly frustrated.

Dave, age fifty-nine, had been married to Marge for thirty-six years. He was a successful realtor and worked hard in his business. One Sunday, while showing a house to a client, he developed a severe chest pain which traveled down his arm. He began to sweat, and he vomited. He was rushed to the hospital, where an EKG confirmed that he had had a heart attack. He was transferred to the coronary care unit and spent six days on a monitor. After some initial difficulty stabilizing the rhythm of his heart, he progressed sufficiently to be transferred to the general floor. Fourteen days later, he was discharged to his home for a recommended six-week convalescence. After this period had elapsed, he was given permission to return to work, though on a somewhat reduced scale. He had occasional chest pains, which responded to nitroglycerin tablets.

The thought of sexual activity had entered Dave's mind on several occasions. He had very mixed feelings about it. He did not wish to do anything that might cause another heart attack, or perhaps even death, but on the other hand, he did not wish to give up that particular pleasure. Marge was quite willing to have sexual intercourse but worried that it might be harmful to her husband. She never discussed these fears with him. At his next office visit, he asked about sexual activities and was told to proceed.

One evening he and Marge engaged in their usual foreplay, followed by coitus. During penetration Dave developed a chest pain, and his erection rapidly faded. Nitroglycerin relieved his discomfort. No further sexual activity was attempted for six weeks. The next time Dave made advances, Marge was frightened that he might harm himself. She refused to proceed, which frustrated Dave and made him mildly angry. At his next office visit, his physician made several suggestions. Dave was advised not to attempt intercourse for at least two hours after eating and to have Marge in the female superior position so that he would expend less physical energy. Dave followed these instructions, and the sexual act was successfully completed. Dave and Marge now have intercourse almost as frequently as before his heart attack occurred.

Studies reveal that few men resume their normal sexual habits after a heart attack. Most have intercourse less frequently, and some abstain altogether. In addition, many men find themselves impotent out of fear. But is this fear justified? Does intercourse impose a significant strain on the heart? It has been demonstrated that during intercourse the heart rate and oxygen consumption increase, and blood pressure rises. Physical demands peak at orgasm and decline slowly but steadily thereafter. Intercourse requires an average energy expenditure of approximately 150 calories. One can assess the physical work imposed by monitoring the heart rate, which is an indirect measurement of oxygen consumption. The pulse averages approximately 120 beats per minute at the time of orgasm. While this may seem to be a rather brisk rate, there is actually no more oxygen consumed than if one had quickly climbed two flights of steps.

A cardiologist, a resident training in cardiology, and an intern had a discussion concerning whether sexual intercourse was work or pleasure. The cardiologist said that in his opinion, sexual intercourse was approximately 60 percent work and 40 percent pleasure. The resident physician suggested that his experience was different; he considered intercourse to be approximately 40 percent work and 60 percent pleasure. Solely out of courtesy, they asked the lowly intern his thoughts on the matter. Having spent most of the past months doing petty jobs for his mentors, he replied, "You're both wrong. Intercourse is one hundred percent pleasure, because if there was any work associated with it, I would be doing it for both of you."

Is it justifiable to worry about death during intercourse? In a Japanese study of 5,559 cases of sudden death, 34 were noted to have occurred during sexual intercourse, but only 18 of these were attributed to heart disease.[1] Twenty-seven of the 34 deaths occurred in association with an extramarital affair, which certainly could be expected to impose more stress on the male.

One medical examiner has noted a pattern for these males who die during intercourse. The man is usually married and is with a woman not his wife in unfamiliar surroundings. He has recently consumed a large meal that included alcohol.

If a man does have a borderline tolerance to physical stress, he may improve his condition by involving himself in a physical fitness program outlined by his physician. Exercises can increase the performance of his heart. In addition, a male should avoid any techniques that he believes are too physically taxing. For example, he may be more comfortable lying on his back with his partner straddling him. In this position, the female performs most of the movement and the male does less thrusting. He certainly should avoid the more exotic positions, particularly if they demand that he support his partner's weight.

If the patient and his physician wish, the activity of the heart can be monitored during intercourse. The patient wears a portable electrocardiogram device that tape-records his heartbeat and can later be studied in the doctor's office. However, this is generally not necessary for the average male heart patient.

In summary, death during intercourse is unusual and should not be feared by heart patients, who should freely discuss their anxieties with their physicians and follow any advice they are given. The vast majority of heart patients should be able to resume normal sexual activity after an appropriate period of convalescence.

Masturbation

> *I would rather have my ignorance than another man's knowledge because I have got so much more of it.*
>
> —Mark Twain

Masturbation has been condemned throughout the ages. Some believe that this proscription has its roots in the Bible. The Book of Genesis relates that Onan utilized withdrawal as a means of contraception. This wasteful "spilling of the seed" infuriated God, who therefore struck Onan dead. Hence the term "onanism," or wasting of the semen, has become synonymous with masturbation.

During the eighteenth century, masturbation was thought to cause insanity and fatal illness. Masturbation was so ill-regarded that some men who could not desist actually committed suicide. At that time, it was believed that prevention was the only way to avoid the torments that were certain to follow masturbation. Some physicians of the day advocated cutting the nerves that lead to the penis in order to prevent erections. The fact that the male would then be impotent was acceptable, since it meant that he had been spared far greater distress. In

Europe, between 1800 and 1850, a plethora of instruments was designed to prevent masturbation. Many of these were constructed of metal and leather and covered the genitalia so securely that a male could not touch his penis. Other implements took the form of spike-lined rings that fit so snugly over the penis that if an erection occurred, the spikes would dig into the skin. These rings could even be worn at night, so that if an erection should occur while the male was asleep, he would be suddenly awakened. Another device consisted of a metal cage that fit over the penis and permitted erections, but had closely fitting bars, so that it was difficult to grasp the phallus and masturbate. However, as an extra precaution, this device was sold with handcuffs. In the early part of the twentieth century, a nurse invented one of the most surefire devices of all. The male was fitted ino a leather jacket and pants. The pants were lined with steel armor and were so foolproof that urine was allowed to escape through perforated holes in the metal, but a separate trap door in the rear, which was padlocked, had to be released by another individual to permit defecation.[2]

In France, in the 1750s, S. A. Tissot cited masturbation as a cause of impotence. In addition, he suggested that masturbation resulted in such other serious complications as loss of vision, indigestion, and mental illness. Dr. Benjamin Rush, a nationally prominent physician of his time, suggested in 1830 that a great sexual appetite would produce impotence. He stated: "When indulged in, an undue or promiscuous intercourse will produce sexual weakness, impotence . . . and death." H. Boerhaave, a Dutch physician who practiced in the early eighteenth century, warned that "the semen discharged too lavishly occasions a weariness, a weakness, an indisposition of motion, convulsions, dryness, pains in the membrane of the brain, dullness of the senses, tabes dorsalis [syphilis], foolishness, and impotence." The *Boy Scout Manual* of 1945 advised boys to "avoid wasting the vital fluid." Many men of that generation, interestingly enough, now suffer from impotence. One can only speculate as to whether there is a relationship between these sexual attitudes and their problems.

At some time or other, masturbation has been blamed for nearly all of the world's evils. Men have been taught to expect baldness, warts on their hands, and blindness if they masturbate. It is therefore no surprise that impotence has also been attributed to masturbation.

Today, masturbation is an accepted part of our sexual lives, as a survey conducted by *Playboy* magazine demonstrates. Ninety percent of all males interviewed in the survey indicated that they had masturbated at some time in their lives. The highest frequency of masturbation occurred in the group between twenty-five and thirty-four years of age.

Among married men, masturbation has increased since Kinsey's report of the 1940s. Kinsey showed that more than 40 percent of married men between the ages of twenty-six and thirty-five masturbated, with a median frequency of six times a year, while in the 1970s more than 70 percent of married men masturbated, with a median frequency of twenty-four times a year.

The fact that men continue to masturbate during adult life and even when they are married does not indicate that they are sexually deranged or oversexed. Rather, for some it is simply pleasurable, while for others it indicates a lack of other sexual activity. If a man's relationship with his female partner has deteriorated so that intercourse is not part of their life-style, masturbation is a logical sexual outlet.

Despite all the myths and old wives' tales, it can be firmly stated that masturbation does *not* cause impotence. If a man derives more pleasure from masturbation than from intercourse, he may lose interest in sexual relationships. However, it does not affect his ability to have an erection.

It is better to ask some of the questions than to know all of the answers.

—James Thurber

Vasectomy, prostate surgery, circumcision, hernia repair, and castration—these operations represent some of the most commonly performed surgical procedures in the United States today. Almost all men wonder if their sexual life will be the same if they undergo one of these operations. In discussions with patients in the hospital, I have noted that there is a great deal of misunderstanding about this topic.

Vasectomy

Vasectomy is currently one of the most popular forms of birth control. Approximately 750,000 vasectomies were performed in the United States in 1977. Many men fear that this procedure will cause impotence, and avoid having a vasectomy despite the fact that their wives have been counseled to discontinue the use of birth-control pills.

A vasectomy involves removing a portion of the tube that carries sperm away from the testicles. No part of the body involved in erections is affected. But some men have expressed concern that since the sperm produced will have nowhere to go, they will become flooded with sperm. One man described himself as a potential walking sperm bank. In fact, this does not occur. New sperm are produced, but old ones die and are removed by cells that are a part of the cleansing system of the body.

Vasectomy has no negative effects on sexual performance. Following a vasectomy, there are no changes in such areas of sexual functioning as the ease and strength of erections, the time from vaginal penetration to ejaculation, and the strength of the ejaculation.[3]

The frequency of intercourse remains either unchanged or very often increases. Most men and women find intercourse more pleasurable because their concern over a possible pregnancy is now eliminated. Both partners feel they have greater freedom, and many women report an increased ease in achieving orgasm.

Another common misconception shared by both men and women is that, following vasectomy, ejaculation will not occur. In fact, semen is still emitted, but it is free of sperm. There is not a significant change in the volume, color, or odor of the ejaculate.

Many surveys have been conducted among men who have had a vasectomy to determine if they are pleased with their decision.[4] Almost all of these studies show that nearly 100 percent are well satisfied. Many men describe themselves as "sexier" following this procedure.

In short, if both the male and female partner agree to proceed with the vasectomy, and if their relationship is stable, there are rarely any adverse psychological effects.

Prostate Surgery

Operations performed because the prostate is enlarged either from a benign disease or from cancer are among the most common surgical procedures in this country today, particularly in men over the age of fifty. Most men undergoing prostate surgery are quite concerned about their ability to function sexually after they recover. One of the oldest patients known to have undergone this procedure was a hundred and five years old, and being mentally alert, even he had questions concerning his sexual abilities.

Today, most prostate operations are performed transurethrally, which means that a special instrument called a resectoscope is inserted in the penis and the prostate is trimmed away. No skin incision is made. Following this procedure, men are generally not impotent. A man who has been functioning normally prior to this procedure usually continues to do so. A man who has had difficulty achieving an erection preoperatively may well continue to do so postoperatively. Many of these patients tend to use the surgical procedure as an excuse to avoid further coitus. Sometimes a patient's partner is not interested in resuming sexual intercourse, and the male will rationalize this predicament by blaming it on his surgery.

Sometimes the prostate is removed by making an incision in the abdomen, and although impotence has been reported following this type of operation, it is relatively uncommon if the male has been functioning normally prior to surgery. In the experience of some physicians, no one has been impotent after this operation unless he was having difficulty with sex beforehand.

It is important to emphasize that following a prostate operation performed either through the penis or through an incision in the lower abdomen, retrograde ejaculation is almost a certainty. A male will have an erection and orgasm, but no semen will be discharged from the end of his penis. This is because the function of the bladder neck is altered and the semen actually is discharged into the bladder, to be voided at the time of urination. Most men having intercourse are not aware of this so-called "dry" ejaculation because the penis is in the vagina, although it would of course be obvious with masturbation.

It must be strongly emphasized that a "radical prostatectomy," in which the entire prostate gland and seminal vesicles are removed, results in impotence in more than 90 percent of the cases. This operation is reserved for special cases of cancer of the prostate. This is *not* the typical operation one has for simple enlargement of the prostate gland.

Thus, patients who have had the common prostate operation should be able to have an erection, and enjoy the pleasurable sensation of an orgasm, even though they won't have normal ejaculations.

Circumcision

Does circumcision, which involves removal of the foreskin from the penis, cause impotence? Many men feel that it does and therefore avoid the procedure, even when it is medically indicated. In fact, a circumcision does not usually cause any problem with erections. If an excessive amount of foreskin is removed, a patient may experience discomfort when he has an erection, and this could result in his avoiding intercourse. However, this situation is extremely rare.

Some men feel that if they are circumcised their penis will become less sensitive. There will no longer be a foreskin to provide stimulation to the head of the penis. However, this is a fallacy, since when an uncircumcised male has a full erection, the foreskin is partially retracted and may not extend fully over the glans penis.

Hernia Repair

While a hernia repair itself usually does not cause impotence, there is no doubt that a hernia that is not repaired may interfere with sexual function and may eventually result in erectile difficulty. If the hernia is significantly enlarged, so that a loop of intestine can enter the scrotum, the male may experience pain with coitus and will therefore avoid intercourse. Some individuals who are well informed about the potential complications of a hernia realize that a loop of intestine may become caught and strangulated in the scrotum. This knowledge has made them so fearful that they avoid all sexual activity.

Some men who have a hernia feel that they are disfigured, and hence are embarrassed to have their female partners see them. To avoid this situation, a male may convince himself that he simply can't get an erection and that therefore there is no need to expose himself to a female.

Castration

Castration refers to removal of the testicles. It dates back to antiquity. It was carried out in ancient China, Rome, and Greece for the purpose of creating eunuchs, who served in imperial courts and were often sold as slaves. Many were used as guards in harems, since they were thought to have no sexual interests. As late as the 1700s, many male children in Italy were castrated so that their voices would not change and they could sing in the male choir. Some Scandinavian countries and certain parts of the United States at one time sanctioned castration as a method of controlling sex offenders.[5]

Doctors are often asked whether a man can have an erection if he loses one or both of the testicles. Some-

116

times a testicle is lost by a trauma, such as an automobile or motorcycle accident, or it is removed because of severe infection. When this happens, men are particularly concerned about their sexual capacity, as are their female partners. Fortunately, only one functioning testicle is needed to have a normal erection and, in fact, to be fertile. If a male has had no difficulty achieving an erection before he has lost a single testicle, then there is no physical reason why he would have difficulty afterward. It is conceivable that a male could be so psychologically disturbed that he would become impotent, but this is extremely rare.

A more complex question concerns sexual functioning after the loss of both testicles. This situation may occur either from trauma or disease or may be a part of the medical therapy for cancer of the prostate. Since the testicles produce the bulk of the male hormone testosterone, it is not surprising that many men find themselves impotent following castration.

Fortunately, testosterone can be replaced through medication (though this would not be advisable for patients with prostate cancer since the goal for them is to stop production of this hormone). Many men who became impotent as a result of testosterone deficiency have been successfully treated by replacement of this hormone. This has been demonstrated in eunuchs and in men who are born with testicles that do not produce a normal amount of this important hormone.

However, many men who have lost their testicles have been able to continue having erections. The degree of impotence that follows castration seems to be related to the man's age when the testicles are removed. Older men are less likely to become totally impotent than younger ones. What will happen to a given individual is unpredictable.

It is not readily appreciated even among physicians that following castration the male may be impotent but may not lose his libido or sex drive. This can prove very frustrating since the desire to perform is present but the ability to do so is absent. Criminals who have been convicted of repeated rape have been treated with the female hormone stilbestrol, which effectively renders them impotent. However, many of these men report no decrease in their sex drive.

Penile Length

---

*What matters is not the length of the wand,
but the magic in the stick.*

—Anonymous

Since men compare themselves to others in a number of ways, including athletic ability, financial success, dress, and physical attractiveness, it is not surprising that the length of the penis has been considered by many as an important gauge of masculinity. Nearly every man has wondered at some time whether his penis is too long or too short, both in the flaccid and in the erect state. In the locker room it is not uncommon for men to sneak a peek at other men's organs in order to reassure themselves of their own endowment. Usually this is a man's only way of comparing penis sizes. In our society, penises are treated like income: you don't ask a man how much money he makes or how long his penis is. There is no question that in some men's minds a long penis is associated with increased masculinity and increased facility in pleasing women. Some men have shied away from sexual intercourse because they felt that their phallus was of insufficient length to satisfy a woman, or out of fear that they would be found inadequate in comparison with other males.

Curiosity about penis size is well documented.[6] In 1935, Oliva Dionne, who had fathered quintuplets, was followed into the bathroom at the Congress Hotel in Chicago by curious onlookers who hoped to get a view of what was alleged to be an extraordinarily enlarged phallus. Jokes about Papa Dionne were widespread:

While visiting a fair, Papa Dionne asked to see a prized bull which was very well endowed. "Listen,"

118

he was told, "it's no problem. The prized bull just asked to see you."

Man's concern over penile length is often expressed in humor. A man will rarely seriously discuss whether his penis is long or short, but few hesitate to tell a good joke about the subject:

Attractive woman: "I'm not going to bed with any man unless he has twelve inches!"
Propositioning male: "Sorry, but I'm not cutting off four inches for any woman."

It is widely thought by both men and women that penile length varies tremendously. However, such is not the case. Objective data on penile length in the flaccid and erect states are difficult to come by, not only because there has been little investigation but also because standardized methods of measurement have not been adequately devised. However, Masters and Johnson have made a significant contribution in this area. Their studies showed that in its nonerect state, the normal penis measures between approximately three and one-third inches to just over four inches, with an average of almost three and three-quarter inches. The average erect penis is six inches long, although its length varies from between four and a half to eight inches.

It has been commonly believed that a penis that was large in its flaccid state would show a proportionately greater increase in length when erect than a smaller penis. In fact, the opposite has been demonstrated by Masters and Johnson, who noted that in their erect state, shorter penises showed a slightly greater proportional increase in length than longer ones.

Another erroneous belief held by many is that big penises belong only to physically big men. However, scientific measurements demonstrate that skeletal and muscular development do not necessarily correlate with penis length. In fact, the largest penis in the Masters and Johnson study was approximately five and a half inches long in the nonerect state, even though the patient himself was only five feet seven inches tall and weighed only 152 pounds.

It is interesting to note that when a man looks at his own penis it appears smaller than when it is viewed by someone else or if he looks at its reflection in a mirror. Thus, by simple self-examination one might sell oneself short. That no one really knows the size of the longest and shortest penises is evidenced by the fact that this information does not appear in the *Guinness Book of World Records*. At any rate, it is very unlikely that a woman can detect slight differences in penile length, and the average male should have no fear of being ridiculed because he has a short organ. Thus, it's not what you have, but what you do with it. As the humorist Josh Billings once said, "Life consists not in holding good cards, but in playing those you do hold well."

It is important for men to understand a woman's attitude toward the size of a penis. Do women really derive greater pleasure during intercourse from a man who has a larger penis? And is a large organ necessarily sexually attractive to a female? There is no doubt that some women may associate a large penis with increased masculinity, but most females are more concerned with the overall qualities of their male partner. There are more important factors than size in determining the degree of satisfaction that a woman will derive from intercourse, and these include such variables as the strength of the emotional relationship, the woman's mood, and the overall setting in which the sex act is occurring.

The absolute length of the penis is not critical in determining female satisfaction. This is true because the most sensitive spot for stimulation in the female is near the opening of the vagina. The area farther inside the vagina has very little sensation. Hence a rather short penis may be just as stimulating in the critical area as a supersized one. And it should not be forgotten that the circumference of the penis may be more important in determining sexual stimulation to the female than the length, since a larger diameter may have more effect on the clitoris. Some women may find an overly large penis difficult to accept into their vagina and therefore may have a rather painful and unpleasant experience. This discomfort may be caused either by friction, which may lacerate the lining of the vagina, or by the repeated striking of the head of the penis against the cervix.

If a man does cause his partner significant discomfort because he is overly endowed, he should work with her to find a position or discover a technique that will permit her to enjoy sexual activity.

Men are always hopeful that something can be done to increase the size of the penis, since, in spite of the facts, so many feel that a large penis indicates greater masculinity and potentially better sexual performance. So it is not surprising that some men hope that increasing the frequency of erections will result in an enlargement of their organ. This is based on the notion that other parts of the body, such as certain muscles, will enlarge in men who are physically active or who lift weights. Certain organs of the body are known to enlarge when increased demands are placed upon them. This is true for the kidney when its mate is lost, and is also true for the heart when an increased workload is continually placed upon it. Unfortunately for the male bent on self-improvement, this phenomenon does not apply to the penis. Any increase in size of the erectile tissues is limited by the tissue surrounding it, which happens to form a very firm sheath. So while one may enjoy "exercising" the penis, one should not expect that it will enlarge.

CAN THE PENIS BE LENGTHENED SURGICALLY?

Certain urological procedures have been described for lengthening the penis, but these are generally applicable only to patients who have certain anatomical defects. For all practical purposes there is no simple procedure for lengthening the penis.

Many men have jokingly asked if a penis transplant could be performed. In fact, some of these individuals are only half joking. Heart transplants continue to make headlines, while kidney transplants have become almost routine. And some men are aware that a penis that has been amputated may be capable of reattachment. As discussed previously, most of the amputations that have occurred are caused by accidental trauma or have been intentionally inflicted—by an irate wife, for instance. Despite the miracles of transplantation and the ability to reattach the penis in these situations, a penis transplant today is not a practical matter. Not only would one be confronted with the problem of rejection of the tissue because it is foreign to the recipient, but it is very difficult to imagine who would volunteer to be the donor!

Will the Application of Testosterone Cream Lengthen the Penis?

It has been suggested that applying the male hormone testosterone to the penis will increase its length. It is true that this will cause the penis to grow. It has been used on prepubescent boys who have an abnormally short penis, particularly if surgery on the penis is required for any reason. However, this medication is not without its side effects, and because it is absorbed into the bloodstream, it may cause the growth centers of the bone to fuse, so that a child could end up being of short stature.

The cream should not be used on the adult penis because of hazardous side effects, such as growth of the prostate gland; it is even possible for it to cause the development of a malignancy of this gland. In addition, the testicles may stop their normal production of this hormone if enough of it is absorbed into the bloodstream.

Does the Penis Shrink?

The penis may become temporarily smaller after such exposure to the cold as jumping into an icy swimming pool. It also may shrink temporarily following complete physical exhaustion. With advancing age or following removal of the testicles, which may have been done to treat prostate cancer, the penis may become permanently reduced in size. It has been suggested that following disuse such as occurs in the impotent male, the penis may become smaller. However, if this does in fact occur, the period of inactivity must be considerable—two to four years, or even longer.

Those men who feel that they have been slighted in their endowment should take heart that they do not

suffer from the koro syndrome.[7] Koro refers to an unusual and extreme form of anxiety that leaves the male
with the firm belief that his penis is suddenly shrinking
and will disappear. This condition occurs most often in
southern China and Southeast Asia. Rarely have cases
been reported in Western culture. Of nineteen men included in one study, the age of the patients ranged from
sixteen to forty-five years, with a median age of thirty-
two. Nine of the men were married, eight were single,
one was separated, and one was widowed. Personality
characteristics indicated that these men were shy, self-
effacing, nervous, and not endowed with much intelli-
gence. Some also lacked physical stamina and were emotionally insecure. An analysis of their sexual history
revealed that thirteen of the nineteen patients were
troubled by sexual deprivation, either because they were
single and had no sexual outlet or were too shy or fearful
of contracting venereal disease to attempt intercourse.
Most of the married patients suffered from their wives'
lack of cooperation. All of the patients were very seriously
worried over what they thought was an abnormal sex
drive. In fact, most of them lacked confidence in their
sexual abilities.

The symptoms of this syndrome are most fascinating.
The patients are so genuinely convinced that their penis
is disappearing that they hold it in their hand to keep it
from vanishing. They are afraid to let go. Each episode
of this anxiety attack usually lasts several hours. The
shortest episode described lasted for half an hour, and
the longest, nearly two days. Most of the attacks occurred at night when they were thinking about sex. Four
patients noted that their attack came after masturbation,
and in three patients it followed coitus. Three other
patients developed an attack after hearing about koro.
One patient, a hairdresser, found that his attacks were
produced by the sexual arousal he experienced when he
handled women's hair during his work.

The reason this syndrome is called "koro" is interesting. In Malay, *koro* means "head of a turtle," and some
believe that there is an obvious similarity between the
head of this animal and the head of the penis.

Penis Captivus

When they are teenagers, most males hear about a peculiar sexual difficulty called penis captivus. This refers to the inability to withdraw the penis from the vagina either during or just after intercourse. An article by Egerton Y. Davis, which appeared in the *Philadelphia Medical News* of December 4, 1884, describes the condition.

When in practice at Pentonville, England, I was sent for about 11:00 p.m. by a gentleman whom, on my arriving at his house, I found in a state of great perturbation, and the story he told me was briefly as follows:

At bedtime, when going to the back kitchen to see if the house was shut up, a noise in the coachman's room attracted his attention and, going in, he discovered to his horror that the man was in bed with one of the maids. She screamed, he struggled, and they rolled out of bed together, and made frantic efforts to get apart, but without success. He was a big burly man over six feet, and she was a small woman, weighing not more than ninety pounds. She was moaning and screaming, and seemed in great agony, so that after several fruitless attempts to get them apart, he sent for me.

When I arrived, I found the man standing up and supporting the woman in his arms, and it was quite evident that his penis was tightly locked in her vagina, and any attempt to dislodge it was accompanied by much pain on the part of both. It was, indeed a case "De cohesione in coitu." I applied water, and then ice, but ineffectively, and at last sent for chloroform, a few whiffs of which sent the woman to sleep, relaxed the spasm, and relieved the captive penis, which was swollen, livid, and in a state of semierection which did not go down for several hours, and for days the organ was extremely sore. The woman recovered rapidly, and seemed none the worse.

The explanation for penis captivus is not known. However, two popular theories are found in the medical literature. One is that the vagina contracts and locks the penis so that it cannot be withdrawn, and the other is that the muscles of the pelvis go into spasm and prevent withdrawal. Some men have actually avoided sexual intercourse because of fear of penis captivus. Some have worried over the embarrassment they would suffer if they had to be taken to the hospital still engaged in the coital position, in order to be separated by a doctor.

One cannot minimize the psychological impact this would have if it were to occur. But the fact of the matter is that penis captivus is a myth. The medical literature fails to document a bona fide case. The description above, while it certainly sounds authentic, was in fact contrived by one of the greatest physicians of all times, Sir William Osler, using the pen name of Egerton Y. Davis. Apparently, Osler wrote this case as part of a plan to embarrass another physician with whom he did not get along.

Many physicians have regarded the facts of this case as real and hence have perpetuated the myth within the medical profession. The lay public, having heard of this condition, has also kept the idea alive.

Venereal Disease

Venereal disease is on the increase, particularly among younger adults. Despite a massive effort by the U.S. Public Health Service to educate the public and thereby control the spread of the disease, it still flourishes. Men who contract venereal disease have many concerns they relate to their doctors. First, they want to know whether the disease can be treated and cured; secondly, those who have had an extramarital affair worry about whether or not they have passed it along to their spouse. They are anxious to know what to tell their wife and are always hopeful that she can somehow be treated surreptitiously, perhaps by putting pills in her coffee. In addition to these concerns, many men fear that they will lose their sexual potency. While there are many types of venereal disease, the most common are gonorrhea, syphilis, and herpes progenitalis.

GONORRHEA

Gonorrhea is primarily an inflammation of the urethra, the lining of the penis, through which urine and semen pass. The first symptom is usually a thick discharge that begins two to seven days after sexual contact. In addition, the male may experience burning when he urinates and an itching sensation inside the penis. The diagnosis can be established through standard laboratory tests, and treatment is readily available in the form of penicillin. For those allergic to this drug, there are other antibiotics that are efficacious. Those males and females who are sexually active with more than one partner should be aware that while gonorrhea is usually very apparent in the male, a female may harbor the infection and be totally unaware of it.

SYPHILIS

Syphilis is caused by a distinctive bacteria called a spirochete (*Treponema pallidum*). The disease first becomes noticeable approximately two to four weeks after sexual exposure. The male will notice a painless skin lesion, called a chancre, which eventually ulcerates and has rather firm margins. It may appear on the penis or, if he has engaged in oral sexual activity, on the tongue or lips. The lesion may be so small that it is overlooked, and it will heal spontaneously without treatment. Because it is not painful and it seems to go away by itself, the male may not know of his problem. However, the infection may progress to a more advanced state. Weeks to months later, a skin eruption may appear, which lasts one to two months. The disease may then become quiescent and there may be no more signs or symptoms. But if it continues into its late stages, many parts of the body will be affected, including the nervous system.

If syphilis is diagnosed early, it is readily treatable by the administration of antibiotics.

Herpes Progenitalis

Herpes progenitalis is caused by a virus (herpes hominis type II); the incubation time after exposure is unknown. Herpes may be, and in fact usually is, transmitted venereally—that is, during sexual contact. This may occur through standard intercourse or through oral-genital contact. However, some people develop herpes without apparent sexual contact. Herpes is characterized by multiple tiny blisters that usually appear on the foreskin and the head of the penis. These blisters may ulcerate and heal spontaneously. Usually there is no significant discomfort other than a slight burning or itching.

Symptomatic treatment may be given in the form of medication applied to the lesions, and there is hope that in the near future a vaccine to prevent the disease will be available.

Do these diseases actually cause impotence? From a physical standpoint, gonorrhea and herpes do not. Syphilis rarely does unless it progresses to its final stage, where it affects the central nervous system and may cause psychosis and paralysis. However, some males who have contracted one of these diseases become so frightened that they avoid sexual contact altogether. Other men are so afraid of becoming infected that they find themselves unable to perform during a sexual encounter.

CHAPTER X
SEXUAL PERFORMANCE AND AGING

It is generally true that most teenagers and men in their twenties and thirties are troubled only infrequently with impotence. They are expected to be sexually capable, and usually are. But what are the sexual abilities of middle-aged and older males?

Sexual Performance in Middle-aged Men

That fellow to me seems to possess but one idea, and that is a wrong one.

—Samuel Johnson

The middle-aged man is stereotypically regarded as being sexually inadequate and unable to satisfy his female partner. Many younger people believe that middle-aged males are not even able to participate in the sexual act. However, the middle-aged man may in fact be better able than his young counterpart to satisfy his female partner sexually.

By middle age, the average man will possess more sexual experiences than a younger man, and he will usually know more sophisticated sexual techniques. He may be more attuned to satisfying his female partner and may engage in more imaginative foreplay. He may utilize different coital positions that are more stimulating and pleasing to the female. He may well be more emotionally involved in his sexual relationships.

In addition, with advancing age certain physiological changes occur that may aid the male in satisfying his female partner. Erections may be prolonged before ejaculation occurs. The period of foreplay may last longer. It has been demonstrated that there is a relationship between the length of foreplay and the orgasmic response among females.[1] If foreplay lasts between one and ten minutes, 40 percent of females reach orgasm most of the time, and 50 percent will climax if foreplay preceding coitus lasts as long as twenty minutes. When foreplay is prolonged beyond twenty minutes, nearly 60 percent will achieve orgasm. In like fashion, there seems to be a relationship between the duration of penetration and orgasm. If penetration takes place less than one minute before ejaculation occurs, 25 percent of women almost always achieve orgasm, whereas 50 percent will do so if penetration lasts between one and eleven minutes. Sixty-five percent will climax if the period of penetration exceeds eleven minutes. When it lasts for more than sixteen minutes, nearly all women achieve orgasm.

Since most middle-aged men can maintain an erection without ejaculation for a longer period of time than younger men, they may use this to advantage and achieve penetration several times in an hour, since they are not, in fact, ejaculating each time.

Hence the sexual life in the middle-aged male is far from over; in fact, there may be some truth in the statement that "life begins at forty." [2,3]

It is noteworthy that studies reveal that when sexual relations between a couple do cease, women generally assign the responsibility for the cessation to their male partners. Interviews with men show that they also believe themselves to be the party responsible for the discontinuation of sexual activity.

Sexual Performance in Older Men

> *To know how to grow old is a master work of wisdom, and one of the most difficult chapters in the great art of living.*
> —Frederic Amiel

Now that both men and women live longer than ever before, it is perhaps inevitable that preconceived notions exist concerning the sexual life of our senior citizens. Usually the older male is thought to have no sexual desire, and therefore it is assumed that he does not partake in sexual activity. If he is sexually active, some will regard him as a "dirty old man." Sometimes when an older man mentions his continuing sexual ability, people merely think that he is engaging in wishful thinking.

The "golden years" of marriage have not been traditionally regarded as a time of sexual fulfillment. This period in a couple's relationship has been characterized by infrequent sexual activity. Often there is mutual disappointment because sexual enjoyment is lacking. When intercourse does occur, it is often treated in a monotonous fashion. The male may find that even when he does attempt to perform sexually, he is not the same man he once was. This disappointment may lead to heightened anxiety and eventual failure to achieve any erection at all.

Many aging men feel it is inevitable that they will become impotent. Many wives also expect a decrease in sexual activity on the part of their husbands as they age. Unfortunately, some physicians are misinformed about sex and aging, and they reinforce this belief. But loss of erection is not necessarily caused by the aging process. Men continue to have intercourse in their eighth, ninth, and tenth decades. One study demonstrated that in the seventh decade more than 65 percent of males retained their coital potency, and in the eighth decade, more than 40 percent did so.[4]

Kinsey's study involved more than 14,000 males, but only slightly more than 100 men above the age of sixty were included, thus seriously underrepresenting older individuals. Kinsey noted that at age sixty, 80 percent of men were still capable of sexual intercourse, but at eighty, only 25 percent could still perform. Masters and Johnson state unequivocally that the male's sexual ability wanes as he grows older. Interestingly, they note that if a male is very active sexually in his earlier years, he is more likely to continue to be active in later years.

A study carried out at the Duke University Center for the Study of Aging and Human Development involved 123 men.[5] Eighty percent of the men who were in good health continued to be interested in sexual activity. However, the proportion of older men who continued to engage in intercourse declined with age. Approximately 67 percent of men in their early sixties were still active sexually, but at age eighty, this fell off to approximately 20 percent. Thus, the study shows that older men do not necessarily lose interest in sex, and many continue to function actively. Our society should no longer view these men as abnormal but should encourage them, for it opens up another avenue of pleasure for older men.

As a male grows older, certain alterations in sexual functioning do occur, however. If the male and his female partner understand these changes, sexual fulfillment may still be realized. Masters and Johnson have depicted many of these sexual changes. After age fifty, a man takes longer to achieve an erection. Partial erections may be achieved and, with further stimulation, can become complete erections. The duration of ejaculation decreases from between four and eight seconds to approximately three seconds. The volume of the ejaculate is reduced from approximately one teaspoon to less than half that amount. The force with which the semen is expelled decreases, so that it is projected from the end of the penis a distance of only two to twelve inches instead of twelve to twenty-four. The time from erection to ejaculation may be increased, and hence a female may be pleasantly surprised that she now has more time to enjoy multiple orgasms. Following ejaculation, the penis becomes soft much more quickly. Before the age of forty, it is not uncommon for this to take several minutes, but after the age of fifty it may occur within a few seconds. The time before the next erection can be achieved is prolonged. With aging, the penis does seem to become less sensitive. Thus, an older male may require more vigorous stimulation in order to achieve an erection and to maintain it, and an overly stretched vagina may not be stimulating enough for older males. In extreme cases, the vagina can be tightened by a surgical procedure.

Research has been done that correlates age and male erectile responsiveness.[6] A comparison of men between the age of nineteen and thirty with those between ages forty-eight and sixty-five reveals that the younger group responds with an erection rate that is 5.8 times faster than that of the older group. Therefore, the male should expect a decrease in penile responsiveness with age. This in no way means that the pleasure derived from sexual relations will decrease. And it certainly does not mean that an older man is incapable of having an erection; it will just take a little longer.

Is There a Male Menopause?

One of the greatest fallacies concerning male impotence centers around the question of whether there is a male climacteric, or menopause. A few males will have symptoms similar to those experienced by menopausal females, such as nervousness, depression, lack of energy, and sometimes even hot flashes. These men also experience a lack of sexual drive that may be associated with impotence. However, this is an extremely rare occurrence, and most impotence problems in this age group are not physiological but psychological.

In middle-aged women, there are very definite signs of physiological change. These include a decrease in the tone and size of the breasts and genitalia, a loss of feminine bodily contours, some deepening of the voice, and a tendency to grow more body hair. In the male, physiological changes are less apparent. It is true that levels of the male hormone testosterone begin to decrease in the mid-forties. This is most likely a result of a decreased rate of production in the testicles. In addition, the size and weight of the testicles decrease with age. However, more obvious changes in the middle-aged man occur in his emotional makeup.

A man undergoes many social and personal adjustments at middle age. Family and business responsibilities may be greater than ever before. In addition, men may realize for the first time that many of their early aspirations will not be met. Other men feel that they have gone as far as they are going professionally and financially, and that there is really nothing to look forward to in life. All of these anxieties common to middle age may result in *psychological* impotence.

Many women state that they know their partner is going through a "change of life." But the fact is that this is probably not a physiological change but is, rather, a *psychological* one.

Some men today believe they should be able to perform sexually much like a machine. They expect that foreplay, erections, vaginal penetration, ejaculation, and orgasm will follow in an automatic sequence. Since most bodily functions, including sexual drive, vary from day to day, the chances of not living up to a predetermined standard are significant; therefore there is a great tendency for men—especially those of middle age—to believe that they are sexual underachievers. It is imperative that they and their female partners realize that sexual performance will vary from time to time and that there are no set standards that must be met on every occasion.

One of the greatest barriers to a continuing, healthy sexual life as one ages is lack of knowledge. If the physiological and psychological facts are understood by both the older male and the female, impotence is not likely to occur. Thus, frustration and disappointment over sexual performance need not occur, and with an understanding couple, it will not.

A sympathetic and considerate female partner is one of the most important factors in continuing potency in the male. Men should not assume a defeatist attitude concerning their sexual abilities as they age, but should take heart in the adage that "the older the fiddle, the sweeter the tune."

CHAPTER XI
TREATMENT FOR THE IMPOTENT MALE

There is perhaps no physical condition that is so humiliating, so demoralizing, and so frustrating as impotence. The ability of the penis to erect is a focus for a considerable amount of masculine self-esteem. When impotence persists for any length of time, the patient can become understandably desperate for treatment.

—*Sexual Medicine Today,* June 1978

While couples should always be encouraged to discuss the problem of impotence among themselves and try to resolve any obvious difficulties, this approach in itself is usually not successful. In most cases, couples cannot talk to each other objectively about this problem, and attempts at discussion often result in hostility. The wife may be angry and suspect that her husband is unfaithful. She may be sexually frustrated and feel that her husband does not really care about her. The male, on the other hand, is usually embarrassed and guilty because he can't satisfy his partner. He develops an inferiority complex and may become depressed. An entire marriage or relationship may be threatened.

Reluctance to Seek Treatment

Today, many aspects of sex and sexual functioning have become popular topics of conversation. Men have always enjoyed describing to their friends their sexual conquests, many of which probably represent wishful thinking. And women are now openly discussing whether or not they can have an orgasm or whether they should masturbate during intercourse. Books are readily available that describe sexual technique, including the various positions of coitus that are most pleasurable for the female as well as the best way to enjoy oral sex. Many of these books contain either photographs or detailed illustrations. Yet one rarely, if ever, hears men discuss their inability to get an erection. While a man will ask his closest associates for advice on virtually every matter, including his financial affairs, when it comes to a personal problem such as impotence, he remains mute. When a man does mention the problem it is usually when he is seeking professional advice. Characteristically, he will initially tell the doctor of another, unrelated complaint. He will often speak of some problem with the prostate. Just as he is ready to leave the office he says, "Oh, Doctor, by the way . . ." He is generally uncertain and embarrassed.

Thus, only after presenting a contrived complaint will the patient inferentially bring up the particular sexual topic that has prompted him to make the appointment. It is not that he doesn't truly want help, but simply that he doesn't know how to ask because society has not encouraged him to seek help for his sexual problems. These cover-ups should be discarded. After one has mustered the courage to obtain help, the problem should be discussed frankly and without any reservation.

What Should a Male Expect When He Visits a Physician for Sexual Advice?

The typical male who is having sexual difficulty is reluctant to visit a physician either because he is embarrassed or because he does not know how to bring up his problem. When he finally summons up the courage to seek help, he enters the doctor's office fully expecting to leave with some medication that will immediately solve his problem. And more often than not, he will be very disappointed—not just when he learns that there is no medicine to magically cure impotence, but when he realizes that his physician may not be capable of handling the problem at all.

The typical physician finds himself in a very uncomfortable position. The patient considers him an expert and expects nothing less than expert advice, when in fact the physician may know little more than the patient himself. While this statement may be shocking, there is an explanation for it. Most physicians practicing today received no training specifically designed to deal with sexual problems. When interviewed, most physicians do not try to hide the medical profession's shortcomings in this area. A majority of all physicians who responded to a poll felt that two-thirds of their peers were inadequately trained to work in this area.[1] One-third of the respondents admitted that they themselves were not competent in this area.

Fortunately, in recent years most medical schools have added to their curriculum specific courses in sexual dysfunction. In California, a law that became effective in January 1978 mandates sexual education for all new physicians and surgeons as a requirement for certification. In the future, patients seeking help will be more likely to find their way to a physician who is competent in this area.

In addition to lacking training, many physicians are simply not comfortable discussing sexual matters; they, too, feel embarrassed. Some doctors are simply too busy with other facets of their medical practice to take the necessary time to help solve the patient's complaint. Finally, those doctors who are impotent themselves may erroneously reason that if they can't solve their own problems, they won't be able to help someone else.

No physician should attempt to treat an impotent patient unless he is genuinely interested and adequately trained to do so. And no patient deserves to be dismissed from the office with a simple statement that "It is all in your head" or "Don't worry—it's not serious." It is equally unfair for the patient simply to be given hormone pills, since hormonal deficiency is rarely a cause of impotence. While most patients are willing to take any prescribed medication in the hope that the problem will disappear, this really represents only wishful thinking.

Any patient who consults a physician for a sexual problem should immediately ascertain whether or not the physician is capable of helping him. How can he do that? He should ask the doctor whether he has treated patients with similar problems. While many patients might feel this would be an insult to the physician, they will soon learn that they have, in fact, gained their doctor's respect for being so forthright. Any physician should have both enough self-confidence and sufficient concern for his patients to refer them to another doctor who specializes in this area—and there are many such physicians. Some are known as sexual therapists.

If the patient does not end up in the hands of a bona fide therapist, he may be misdiagnosed and treated for a physical problem when the real difficulty is psychological, or he may be treated for a psychological factor when the true cause is physical. Either error in diagnosis will cause the patient a significant loss of time and money.

In the past, treatment for impotence consisted of some form of psychotherapy and was normally left to a psychiatrist. There have been many cures utilizing this form of therapy. But psychoanalysis is very time-consuming and expensive. More recently, other physicians, including urologists, internists, gynecologists, and sex counselors, working either alone or as a team, have joined in the treatment program. They employ short-term behavioral techniques that stem primarily from the pioneering work of William H. Masters and Virginia E. Johnson.

The Nonsurgical Treatment of Impotence

Masters and Johnson have introduced several revolutionary concepts concerning the treatment of impotence. First, they point out that in a male-female relationship, there is no such thing as an individual patient. Both persons must be treated. Second, any treatment given to one partner must be understood by the other. Finally, the couple is best treated by a dual therapy team. The advantage of using a dual therapy team, which includes a male and female therapist, one of whom is a physician, is that two opinions are readily available in the management of each case, and each partner has someone of the same sex present to help understand his or her particular sexual difficulty. In sexual counseling, it is emphasized that couples must understand that sexual intercourse is a joint concern and that both people's feelings must be taken into account. Sex is something that both partners are to enjoy, and if a particular sexual activity is offensive to an individual, it should not be forced upon him or her. In short, intercourse is something that partners do *with* each other and not *to* each other. This method of treatment is not confined to any age group. The only real requirements are general good health, an earnest desire to be helped, and, most importantly, a cooperative partner.

Masters and Johnson point out that just as you cannot make a female have an orgasm, you cannot force a male to have an erection and ejaculate. Only through mutual help and cooperation will these occur. A male who has difficulty achieving an erection soon becomes fearful of future failure. It is often difficult for the female partner to appreciate the depth of this fear. The male begins to observe himself to see whether he can get an erection, whether he can penetrate, and finally, whether he can ejaculate. This self-observation is very distracting and lessens the likelihood of having a successful erection. Furthermore, after repeated failures, the female partner also begins to observe the male, and she becomes distracted. Thus, it is the relationship that must be treated. Masters and Johnson stress that they do not have to teach a male how to get an erection, since this is a natural function. What they have to do is help remove his anxiety and fear of failure.

What to Expect When You Visit a Sexual Therapist

Most males who are referred for sexual therapy have no idea what to expect, and some decide not to proceed out of fear. Some basic information may help alleviate this concern and encourage men to seek the help they deserve. While there have been many variations on Masters and Johnson's original technique, and although each therapist has his or her own unique style of treatment, some generalizations can be made.

Every therapist will want a detailed medical history in order to ensure that there are no physical reasons for erectile failure. All medications that are being taken will be reviewed to see whether they are causing the difficulty. An explicit sex history is taken to uncover the specific sexual inadequacy and any areas of stress and conflict. This information will also reveal whether there are any psychological components contributing to the problem. A physical examination will be performed or a report will be requested from the referring doctor. Particular attention will be paid to whether the genitalia are of normal size and whether there is any evidence of male hormone deficiency. The presence or absence of pulses in the legs will be determined to make certain that there is an adequate blood supply to the genitalia. A prostate examination will also be done.

Certain laboratory tests may be requested. In addition to a general blood count, a blood sugar may be done to exclude the possibility of diabetes. The level of the male hormone testosterone may or may not be determined. This is not always necessary.

During the sessions, a general introduction to male and female anatomy is given. Scientific facts about sexual functioning are discussed. Along with verbal instruction, models and movies may be used.

The length of the treatment program is variable, and will be individualized, depending on the patient's particular problem. Some therapists and their patients meet on a daily basis for several weeks, while others may meet only once a week for several months. If a male is not married, he is encouraged to bring a female with whom he has a strong emotional relationship.

A great deal of confusion exists concerning the therapist's use of surrogate partners. Some males enter therapy believing that they will be provided with a female partner who will teach them how to have an erection. In fact, surrogates are rarely used. Any physical contact that does occur takes place only with the female whom the patient brings.

The couple is given specific instructions on how to make physical contact once they are alone. At first, this contact is confined to pleasurable stroking and massage, though initially the genital area of each partner is excluded and no coitus is permitted. During this time, the man and woman tell each other what gives them the most pleasure. If the man does achieve an erection, intercourse is still forbidden. The erection is positive reinforcement and assures the male that he is indeed capable. After using only these stroking techniques for a specific period of time (which varies from couple to couple), the pair will be told by the therapist to try actual coitus, but in a specific manner. The female is told to assume the superior position and to insert the penis into the vagina herself, thus relieving the male of this responsibility. The success rate of couples following these instructions is very impressive, with Masters and Johnson reporting a better than 80 percent improvement in cases of secondary impotence.

Not all investigators have been able to duplicate the impressive results of Masters and Johnson, but it must be remembered that this team's cases are carefully selected and that their patients are referred by other physicians only after the impotent male has tried another form of therapy for at least six months. Thus, they are treating only highly motivated individuals. A major disadvantage is that Masters and Johnson require two weeks of participation in their program, and not every man and woman can fit such a schedule into their lives. In addition, the cost—including travel and accommodations—is prohibitive for most people. However, many medical schools around the country now have sex clinics, and the sessions are spread out over several months. Office treatment may be combined with at-home practice sessions.

It is important to exercise caution when selecting one of these sex clinics, for there are now more than 5,000 in operation in the United States. Since licensing is not generally required, anyone can become an authority on sex simply by hanging out a shingle. It is imperative that males or females seeking sexual help find themselves a competent and ethical sexual counselor. A great deal of time and money have been wasted—and damage done—by advisers who are not adequately trained. It should again be emphasized that at no time will a reputable sex therapist observe the male or his female partner in sexual foreplay or intercourse. If this is suggested, a new therapist should be sought. Unfortunately, some therapists have satisfied their own voyeuristic needs by insisting on observation. And it is not uncommon to find that women who have sought help alone because their sexual relationships have been inadequate have ended up being seduced by a male counselor. Unless one has been given a specific reference, it is best to seek professional advice before choosing a therapy team or clinic.

All reputable therapists keep their records strictly confidential. The cost of treatment varies tremendously, depending upon the therapist and the geographical location. One should ascertain ahead of time what the fee will be.

Hypnosis

Another form of therapy currently in use is hypnosis. This is utilized to reveal unconscious conflicts concerning sex that might cause impotence. Often sexual experiences, such as masturbation, for which the patient was punished during childhood are brought out. Hypnotherapy sessions allow a patient to express his own anxieties concerning erections and intercourse. They are designed to show the patient how his negative attitudes developed and what he can do to restructure them in a positive way. Ego-strengthening suggestions are made in order to improve the man's self-image.

The following case history demonstrates the usefulness of hypnosis:

The patient, age twenty-five and single, stated that he had been impotent all his life and had never had intercourse. For the past seven to eight years he had been trying desperately to do so. During treatment, he remarked that "it hurts and I shy away." Through hypnosis it was learned that at an early age his brother had performed fellatio upon him. His brother instructed him to "relax, it's just like having a woman's pussy slide over it." During the oral sex act his penis was badly bitten by his brother. It became evident that he associated this damage with potential injury from a vagina. In addition, he had guilt feelings about his adolescent homosexual experience.

After these anxieties had been pointed out and resolved, he was able to engage in intercourse without difficulty. The time spent in therapy prior to his first successful coitus was only six hours. The total time in treatment was thirteen hours.[2]

The advantage of hypnotherapy is that it is relatively short-term. In one study evaluating the effectiveness of hypnosis, the total treatment time averaged just over twelve hours. In addition, it appeals to many individuals because of its mystique. But how successful is hypnosis in the treatment of impotence? There have been few large-scale, controlled scientific studies. Some physicians claim better than 90 percent success, but the medical literature suggests approximately 55 percent overall improvement through hypnosis.

Hormonal Treatment

What about hormonal treatment? Men are aware that women who are passing through the menopause profit from the administration of estrogen hormones. Therefore, many conclude that there must be a hormone available to resurrect a fallen phallus. Great controversy exists within the medical profession concerning the usefulness of male hormones for the treatment of impotence. Some experts feel that hormones have no place in the treatment of impotence unless there is a definite deficit of the hormone in the individual. Others note that patients do increase both their general interest in sex and their erectile ability following the administration of hormones, either in the form of a pill or of injections. Research is currently under way to try to determine the true effectiveness of hormone therapy.

A male's testosterone level is easily determined by a single blood test, which may be done before he takes a hormonal drug. A physician's guidance is required if this therapy is to be tried.

Treatment for Uncontrollable Ejaculation

Premature ejaculation in younger men should be viewed differently from that in older, more experienced males. Unfortunately, all too often when young men mention their concern about uncontrollable ejaculation to a physician, they are simply told, "Don't worry, you'll grow out of it." Instead, the younger individuals should receive reassurance. The doctor and patient should frankly discuss the expectations of each young man, since these individuals so often set themselves unrealistic goals, such as expecting to sustain active thrusting for fifteen to twenty minutes. It is very unlikely that this goal will be achieved, since often the female partner is not well known to the man and there exists no strong emotional relationship between them. For this reason, it is not likely that the female would be willing to participate in the "squeeze technique," which will be described shortly.

Since the young male will probably not have a female partner to help him develop ejaculatory control, he will have to train himself. This can be accomplished by recommending that the patient masturbate, but stop just prior to ejaculation. The male will thereby learn to sustain an erection with stimulation but without quickly ejaculating. If, indeed, the young man finds that even after practice he continues to have repeated episodes of uncontrollable ejaculation with multiple partners, he should consider seeking advice from a qualified physician.

Many remedies to increase control and prolong the erection before ejaculation have been tried. Some men wear condoms, while others apply local anesthetics to the glans penis. Still others masturbate prior to intercourse, which may help, but certainly all of these techniques decrease the overall pleasure for the male. Certain medications—namely, the MAO inhibitors and the phenothiazines—may be beneficial but should never be taken without a doctor's management. There are better ways to control ejaculation.

Masters and Johnson have reported nearly 100 percent success in utilizing the so-called squeeze technique. Using this method, the male is instructed to signal his partner when ejaculation is imminent. He withdraws his penis from the vagina, and she then places her thumb on the bottom of the penis and her first and second fingers on the top of the penis near its end; then she squeezes for approximately three seconds. The erection will disappear. When the penis again becomes erect, the female inserts it in the vagina while she is in the superior position. She is therefore responsible for assuring proper position and relieves her partner of this potentially anxiety-producing maneuver. Thrusting by the male should be active enough to maintain an erection but not to cause him to ejaculate. **The penis is removed from the vagina and squeezing is applied when the male** again signals his partner that ejaculation is forthcoming. The procedure can be repeated until an erection has been maintained long enough to satisfy both partners.

A new modification of the squeeze technique has been introduced by Masters. The male applies pressure to his urethra, the tube through which urine and semen are normally conducted. The pressure is applied underneath the scrotum by squeezing the urethra, which can easily be felt, between the fingers. This technique inhibits ejaculation if the male has not reached such a state of excitation that ejaculation is inevitable. The advantage of this method is that the penis may be retained within the vagina while pressure is applied.

Another successful method involves the female's stimulating the male to a point just short of ejaculation, and then letting the erection fade. This process is repeated over and over until the male can sustain an erection for a considerable period of time without ejaculating. It is essential that penile stimulation cease before the male reaches a point at which ejaculation is inevitable.

There are also other ways of dealing with uncontrollable ejaculation. Men who ejaculate before their female partner achieves an orgasm find that if they repeat the sexual act as soon as they are able, the period of time before they ejaculate again will probably be prolonged. If the male can keep his partner sexually stimulated while waiting for his next erection, he and she may be very satisfied.

Many creams are being promoted that are said to sustain an erection. These contain an anesthetic and are generally not highly effective. They have one major disadvantage, which is that the cream may do more to anesthetize the vagina than to help the male prolong his erection. In addition, the male may complain that since his penis is less sensitive, intercourse is less pleasurable.

Other men will resort to wearing a condom, which decreases the stimulation of the penis during thrusting. However, this is generally not satisfactory to the male or the female. Many men do not like putting one on, and many women consider them unnatural and want the real thing.

One technique that is somewhat helpful is for the female to assume the superior position. This enables her to carry on most of the physical activity, and because the male is not doing the thrusting, the probability of rapid ejaculation is decreased.

Because of the very high cure rate reported using the squeeze technique, men who suffer from uncontrollable ejaculation should be encouraged to try it on their own or to seek a professional explanation of the technique. It is my experience that the male and female have more confidence in using this technique if it is explained to them by a physician or sex counselor.

Surgical Treatment

> *Knowing is not enough; we must apply.*
> *Willing is not enough; we must do.*
>
> —Goethe

Before noting the significant strides that have recently been made in the surgical treatment of impotence, let us look to researchers of the past.[3] The work of Ancel and Bouin in France in the early 1900s, and that of Steinach in the 1920s, suggested that vasectomy promoted sexual rejuvenation. In 1936, Niehans noted the positive effects of this procedure in correcting impotence in humans. In 1918, Voronoff, a Parisian, declared that youth could be restored by transplanting a portion of monkeys' testicles into man. That same year, Lespiansse, a professor of genitourinary surgery at Northwestern University, treated male impotence by implanting slices of human testicles taken from fresh cadavers into a small incision made in the abdomen of the sexually inadequate male.

Stanley, a physician working with a captive population at San Quentin Prison in California, published a paper in 1922, citing 1,000 testicular implant surgical procedures that had been performed on 656 patients. Unlike Lespiansse, who used human testicular tissue, Stanley chose the testicles of goats, rams, boars, and deer. The testicles from these animals were cut into strips with a knife in sizes suitable for the filling of a pressure syringe. The testicular substance was then injected by force underneath the skin of the abdomen. Stanley noted no significant difference in the effects produced by the testicular material taken from the various animals. Today, testicular implantation, using either human material or that obtained from animals, is not considered a valid procedure.

It is well known that necessity is the mother of invention. This explains why the U.S. Patent Office has issued approximately a hundred patents for devices that are designed to improve the sexual performance of the male.[4] Many of these devices consist of splints to support the penis or rings that fit onto the base of the penis in order to decrease the outflow of blood and thereby cause an erection.

Recent work has focused on trying to create a natural-appearing erection, and the most modern techniques involve placing a prosthesis within the phallus. The idea of having something rigid in the penis is corroborated in nature. As we noted earlier, some mammals have a bone in the penis, although humans do not. In the walrus this bone is two feet long, while in the whale it may reach six feet. Among the earliest substances used to impart rigidity to the penis was a patient's own rib cartilage. But now modern science has provided us with silicone and other synthetic materials.

Today, there are two general types of prostheses in use. One causes a permanent semirigidity in the penis, while the other allows the penis to be stiffened and relaxed depending on need. The first type of device is generally placed within the erectile tissue on the top side of the penis. It was first introduced in the 1960s. There are currently several different models available; all of them make the penis rigid enough to permit its introduction into the vagina and ensure successful intercourse. The penis is, however, by no means as rigid as it is with a normal erection. In order to minimize cosmetic deformity, these prostheses are usually held against the abdominal wall by tight-fitting jockey shorts or by an athletic supporter.

A major innovation in the area of penile prostheses has been made by Dr. F. Brantley Scott of Baylor University. Dr. Scott's device may be inflated and deflated by the patient, using a small pump that is placed alongside one testicle inside the scrotum. Excellent results have been obtained with this device, which some have nicknamed the "erector set." It was first used in humans in 1973. Dr. Scott's patients have ranged in age from twenty-one to eighty. Almost all of them have been impotent as a result of physical illnesses or certain major surgical procedures. Following implantation of the inflatable penile prosthesis, patients are advised not to have intercourse for approximately three weeks. If a patient was having successful orgasm, though no erection, prior to receiving the device, the orgasmic sensation is retained. And a few patients who could not have an orgasm before have been able to do so after surgery, since they can now have an erection that permits penetration of the vagina.

No surgical procedure is without its potential complications, and the implantation of penile prostheses is no exception. There are advantages and disadvantages to each type of device, and certain problems that are common to both. The shared problems include the possibility of infection, in which case the device will have to be removed. However, after the infection has cleared up, a new prosthesis can be inserted. Another difficulty occurs if a prosthesis has been improperly fitted. If it is too long, it could cause discomfort either to the male or to the female; if it is too short, it could prevent effective intercourse. However, since the devices are now available in varying widths and lengths, sizing problems are becoming less common. The device may erode through the skin, which would necessitate its removal. The prosthesis may fracture (this usually occurs during intercourse) and have to be replaced.

The inflatable penile prosthesis has several advantages over the noninflatable type. It seems to give a firmer erection. Also, since the penis is extended only when the device is voluntarily inflated, there is no problem with concealment. In fact, in the flaccid state, the presence of the device is not discernible. On the other hand, there are several disadvantages to this model. There may be a mechanical failure in the pump, or the fluid that is inside the device and is used to distend it to create an erection may leak. The inflatable device is also more expensive and generally requires more surgical skill to put it in place.

The semirigid device is not perfect, either. The disadvantages of the semirigid prosthesis include the fact that it is more difficult to conceal. It is more likely to erode through the skin than the inflatable model, and may have to be removed. Also, the female can feel the presence of this semirigid device, and she may find it disturbing.

It should be apparent that with either of the above

devices in place, a man is ready for action at any time. The duration of intercourse is only limited by his, or his partner's, fatigue.

In May 1978, the manufacturer of the inflatable penile prosthesis, The American Medical Systems, Inc., compiled data from the 17 physicians around the United States who have had the most experience with this device. A total of 745 separate implantation procedures had been performed by these surgeons.

First, the causes of the patients' impotence were listed:

Diabetes	229
Vascular disease	78
Unknown organic causes	72
Spinal cord injuries	66
Pelvic trauma	59
Post-prostatectomy	59
Psychologic factors	54
Radical surgery	42
Peyronie's disease	26
Priapism	10
Genital trauma	8
Other	42

The study grouped the patients thus:

Age	No. of implants
Under 20	1
20–29	47
30–39	84
40–49	174
50–59	207
60–69	199
70–79	30
Over 80	3

The overall success rate was 93.3 percent.

The semirigid device has been utilized for patients with impotence due to all of the causes listed above. Many surgeons claim similar success rates.

A man must fulfill certain requirements in order to be considered a candidate for either type of penile prosthesis. He should have a satisfactory sexual drive and be in generally good health. His penis should have normal sensation when it is stimulated. He should be emotionally healthy. The cause of his impotence should not be amenable to treatment by less formidable methods, such as sexual counseling.

There is an increasing tendency to treat men with psychological impotence by surgical implantation of a prosthesis. If the patient has been properly evaluated and continues to fail sexually after counseling, then some experts have no objection to surgical treatment. Patients must be properly screened so that those with serious psychological illnesses are excluded. In addition, men who have transient forms of impotence, such as those caused by acute anxiety or depression, should be excluded, as well as those who cannot perform with one partner but can with others.

As already noted, impotence may be a serious problem for men of all ages, even older ones. Among the letters received by Dr. Scott from patients desiring a penile prosthesis is the following:

Dear Doctor Scott: I hope you can help me. I am ninety-two years old and recently married my second wife. She is eighty-nine years old and is a virgin. She states that she is not interested, but I truly believe she would like to have sex.

Will a Prostitute Help?

Happiness grows at our own firesides, and is not to be picked in strangers' gardens.
—Douglas Jerrold

Nearly every man who is impotent has wondered at some time whether he might be able to have an erection

151

and successful intercourse with a new partner. And some men feel that a very experienced female, such as a prostitute, might be able to stimulate them sufficiently to be able to perform. These individuals feel that a prostitute knows certain techniques that would ensure a good erection.

However, men whose impotence has a physical cause will not derive any benefit from a prostitute, or from any form of sexual stimulation. Men who are impotent for psychological reasons are no more likely to benefit, since what they most often need is a sympathetic and understanding female partner. Obviously, many prostitutes do not meet this need. The more customers they service in a night, the higher their profits. Therefore, few are willing to spend any time with a male who cannot perform. Patient foreplay, which an impotent male very much needs, usually does not take place during a sexual encounter with a prostitute. Since a prostitute's attitude is strictly businesslike, any man who has difficulty performing may be treated with contempt. Furthermore, the very knowledge that a man is dealing with a professional may impose demands upon him that he cannot fulfill. The male will be more concerned with performance than with enjoyment, and almost certainly will not be able to achieve an erection because of his anxiety.

Some impotent males have wondered whether they might solve their problem by seeking sexual stimulation at a massage parlor.[5] Such establishments have recently sprung up in virtually every major city in the United States. However, few men know what will occur when they go in for a massage. They know even less about the types of individuals who patronize such places.

While differences between massage parlors do exist, most treatments consist of a general body massage, culminating in a "local," which consists of a genital massage, usually lasting no more than five minutes.

An interesting survey characterized the patrons of massage parlors. The typical customer is white, thirty-five years old, and married. He has had at least thirteen years of education but is employed in a lower- or middle-class occupation. He is a regular churchgoer. He has probably come to the massage parlor because he is dissatisfied with his sexual partner or out of curiosity. Personality evaluation reveals that these men generally have high self-esteem and consider themselves personally and sexually well adjusted.

When queried as to whether they came for the massage or the "local," 40 percent of the men interviewed stated that they came for the massage, 40 percent for the "local," and 20 percent for both. Thirty-eight percent of the patrons failed to reach orgasm during the five-minute genital massage.

As a rule, men who frequent massage parlors are not sexually dysfunctional. For those men having sexual difficulties, a massage parlor would be a poor place to try to work out their problems. The climate itself is anxiety-producing, and the genital massage is strictly mechanical. There is no time for the emotional support or encouragement that the impotent male needs.

The Effect of Illegal and Misused Drugs upon Sexual Function

> *I once knew an old manufacturer who said: "All information is false." And, he was right, for almost everything is exaggerated, distorted, or suppressed.*
>
> —André Maurois

Because most impotent men are anxious for a quick cure, it is not surprising that some try to obtain those illegal substances that are so often touted as "miracle drugs." In other instances, a man who is experiencing sexual difficulty might be tempted to try a medicine that is not intended to be used for enhancing sexual function but is alleged to have this benefit. It is unfortunate that sometimes the only information the impotent male has comes from a misinformed friend.

The idea that drugs may enhance sexual pleasure and

performance is not a new one. Roman orgies have been well documented in both literature and art. At such orgies, alcohol and other drugs were freely used, and social and sexual inhibitions vanished.

Do any illegal drugs facilitate sexual performance? Reliable data are hard to come by because few scientific studies have been conducted. However, we do know certain things about the effects of some commonly used illicit drugs on sexual behavior.

MARIJUANA

Marijuana is now widely in vogue in the United States, particularly since the penalties for its use are being relaxed. This drug, which is obtained from the flowering tops of hemp plants, has been used for centuries but has only recently become popular. Many people have claimed that their sexual experience is heightened and their performance improved by smoking marijuana prior to intercourse. This drug does induce a dreamy state in which many ideas freely flow. Perceptions change, and hallucinations may occur. However, its only apparent role in sex may be that in small doses it reduces anxiety, which might otherwise prevent a male from obtaining an erection. It certainly is not a scientifically proved method of increasing either sex drive or erectile ability.

In fact, marijuana may have negative effects. The Indian Hemp Drug Commission of 1894 reported that hemp drugs have "no aphrodisiac power whatever; and, as a matter of fact, they are used by ascetics in this country with the ostensible objective of destroying sexual appetite." [6] The drug does cause a heightened awareness of thoughts and feelings, which may lead to a disinterest in the relationship with a female partner. Therefore, despite the positive effects claimed by some users, marijuana is not a cure for impotence.

HEROIN

Narcotics in general have a deleterious effect upon sexual performance. Most drug addicts are impotent, and many others are unable to ejaculate. When the male is "high," he cannot perform sexually. When he is not high, his basic concern—indeed, his obsession—is where he will get his next fix. Also, there is some evidence that prolonged use of narcotics may lower the level of the male hormone testosterone, which could adversely affect potency.

The initial sensation following the intravenous injection of heroin is pleasant and warm. An erection may occur, but it usually disappears rapidly. Some men experience such total euphoria that they describe their high as being just like an orgasm. This may actually replace the need for those feelings that sexual intercourse would provide. Most addicts report that their frequency of sexual intercourse is less than once a month.

METHADONE

Methadone is now a familiar drug used to withdraw hard-core addicts from heroin and morphine. It usually results in an overall improvement in sexual functioning in addicts. However, it is not of value for the nonaddicted impotent male.

AMPHETAMINES

There is evidence that amphetamines may increase sexual activity. Interestingly, when a male is high on amphetamine, he has little interest in sex. It is only during the withdrawal, or "crash," that sexual interest and performance is heightened. Amphetamine has been experimented with in groups, and sexual activity has often followed. Some males report spontaneous erections after an injection of amphetamine, and many individuals under the influence of the amphetamines describe their sexual experience as being prolonged. Many report an increase in libido as well. However, these drugs are not without harmful side effects. Confusion, hallucinations, panic states, homicidal tendencies, and fatal convulsions may occur. They should not be used as treatment for impotence.

LSD

Among those involved in the so-called drug culture, LSD is not noted for enhancing sexual performance. It may cause sexual hallucinations, but performance is generally made more difficult because the user cannot concentrate on reality long enough to accomplish anything. For every individual who feels that his sexual experience is enhanced, there is another who feels that LSD has detracted from his sexual performance.

COCAINE

Hard-core users of cocaine usually develop sexual difficulties, and impotence is not uncommon. But there is no doubt that some males report that with very intermittent use they experience an increase in sexual pleasure since they seem to be capable of experiencing either prolonged or multiple orgasms.

Cocaine produces an anesthetic effect and has been used by some males as an aid to prolonging intercourse before ejaculation occurs. It is rubbed on the head of the penis just prior to insertion and may permit more vigorous thrusting before a male ejaculates. However, many female partners have experienced trauma to the lining of their vaginas as a result of such prolonged activity.

METHAQUALONE (QUAALUDE)

This drug is used medically either to produce sleep or to sedate people in the daytime. Some patients who have used this medication complain of dizziness and a tingling sensation in their extremeties. Others have developed a skin rash. Overdosage may result in delirium and coma as well as convulsions. Methaqualone has recently been extremely popular, and some users claim prolonged orgasmic experiences. However, not every user has so benefited. At this time, no scientific effect has been proved, and the drug should not be used for the treatment of impotence.

BARBITURATES

This class of drugs is generally not helpful for sexual dysfunction. In small or moderate doses, anxiety may be reduced and inhibitions removed, but in larger doses, one becomes sedated and sexual performance is impaired. Libido is also diminished. Commonly used barbiturates include phenobarbital (Luminal), secobarbital (Seconal), and pentobarbital (Nembutal).

In summary, we do not yet have even one scientifically proved drug that will aid the impotent male (except testosterone for the hormonally deficient male). Data are scarce, and most information is derived from young men who normally should not need any assistance in sexual functioning. Many men perceive that their performance is improved with the use of one or another illegal drug, but it is more likely that their favorable experiences are heavily influenced by their wishes and expectations.

There are several medications used by impotent males that, while not illegal, are misused in that they are not really intended to enhance sexual performance. Some are very common medicines that are beneficial when used for their intended purpose. Rarely do they have any positive effect on sexual functioning.

VITAMIN E

Vitamin E has recently been widely touted as an aid to potency. Experiments have demonstrated that sexual function is reduced in rats totally deprived of vitamin E. When this vitamin is supplied to the deprived rats, their sexual abilities return to normal. However, tests show that increased quantities of vitamin E in the human diet do not increase either libido or potency. There is no scientific evidence that it either increases the general sex drive or facilitates an erection.

MUSHROOMS, TRUFFLES, AND OTHER "APHRODISIACS"

Mushrooms, truffles, oysters, and many other foods have been credited with enhancing sexual performance. None of these claims is considered scientifically accurate. One patient swore to his doctor that his performance was greatly enhanced by eating a sausage pizza. This must be considered a unique experience!

CAFFEINE

Since it is present in coffee, caffeine is one of the most widely ingested drugs in the world. Caffeine is a stimulant and might prove beneficial in improving sexual performance in normally functioning individuals who are otherwise too tired physically or mentally. However, for those suffering from true sexual dysfunction, caffeine has not been demonstrated to have any therapeutic effect.

TOBACCO

Pharmacologically, tobacco does not cause an improvement in sexual drive or erectile ability. However, like any other substance, it may have a psychological effect. It can make a male feel more relaxed or reduce his anxiety.

L-DOPA

Many rumors exist concerning the positive effects of L-dopa on the impotent male. This drug, which is used primarily for the treatment of patients who have Parkinson's disease, has been known to improve sexual performance in certain patients afflicted with this illness. However, interviews reveal that the improvement occurs because the patient is feeling better generally, both psychologically and physically, since many of the symptoms of the disease have been alleviated by use of the drug. Certainly, L-dopa is not a medication to be considered for the general treatment of male impotence.

AMYL NITRITE

The drug amyl nitrite is familiar to many people as a heart medicine. In the past it was used solely for relieving attacks of angina. Many heart patients continue to carry it on their persons. During an attack, a small glass vial wrapped in a fine cloth is crushed in the hand and then immediately inhaled. It has largely been replaced by nitroglycerin.

Amyl nitrite has become an extraordinarily popular sex drug. Some men inhale this medication during sexual intercourse to release inhibitions or enhance orgasm. It definitely causes the blood vessels to dilate and in so doing may, in fact, lessen the firmness of an erection or even delay orgasm and ejaculation. It has become popular among homosexuals because there is some speculation that it may relax the internal anal sphincter, thus facilitating anal intercourse. However, it may also cause a lowering of the blood pressure and an increase in the heart rate, and it poses certain dangers to persons with known or underlying heart disease.

This drug is not without other hazards. Physiologically, it causes relaxation of the smooth muscles of the body and may result in such unpleasant side effects as headaches and pain in the eyes, the latter due to an increase in pressure within the eyeball. It can cause dizziness and a feeling of faintness that may be described as an increase in the intensity of orgasm, but it does not facilitate erections and should be avoided as a means of treating impotence.

SPANISH FLY

Many men and women consider this to be the "wonder drug" for curing impotence. Over the years, great claims have been made for this drug's ability to "turn on" a man or woman.

A pupil of the famous French surgeon Ambroise Paré, wrote an interesting account of an overdose of cantharides:

In 1572, we went to see a poor Argonian man in Provence who was affected by the most horrible and frightful satyriasis one could ever see. The fact is this: he had quartan fever; to cure it he consulted an old sorceress who made him a potion composed of an ounce and a half of nettles and two drams of cantharides, which made him so ardent in the venereal act that his wife swore to us by her God that he had been astride her, during two nights eighty-seven times, without thinking it more than ten . . . and even while we were interviewing him, the poor man ejaculated thrice in our presence.[7]

The active ingredient in spanish fly is cantharidin. This comes from a beetle that is found in central and southern Europe. When the beetle is dried and powdered, it is known as spanish fly. It is an extremely irritating substance when taken internally, and it may indirectly cause an erection.

However, serious side effects of cantharides include severe abdominal pain, frequent and painful urination, and even the passage of some bits of tissue that come from inside the irritated penis. It can be a very dangerous drug and should not be tried.

GINSENG

Another substance claimed to be an aphrodisiac is ginseng. Ginseng grows wild in many areas of the United States and is sold in drug and health-food stores. It is also found in soap and tea. In central Wisconsin, the ginseng industry flourishes, growing approximately 95 percent of all the cultivated ginseng in the United States. Many claims are made by those who believe in its efficacy. However, there is no real evidence that it increases the sexual drive or the ability to attain and maintain an erection.

NUX VOMICA

There is one medication to be avoided that deserves special mention. Rumors abound about the effectiveness of nux vomica as a sexual stimulant. This drug comes from the seeds of a tree native to India. Its principal ingredient is strychnine, which was introduced into Germany in the sixteenth century as a pesticide to eliminate rats and vermin. Because it is still used as a rat poison, one occasionally hears of the accidental death of a child who has ingested a "rat biscuit."

Strychnine has an excitatory effect on all portions of the central nervous system. It is a powerful convulsant and causes rapid contraction of the muscles. Strychnine poisoning is characterized by stiffness of the face and neck muscles. Any sensory stimulation, whether auditory, visual, or tactile, produces a violent convulsion in which the body is arched, so that in extreme form, when lying down, only the back of the head and the heels of the patient may be touching the ground. Because the diaphragm, the muscle that controls breathing, is in a state of full contraction, respiration ceases and death ensues.

Clearly, any sexual stimulation that might be derived

is overshadowed by the potentially dangerous side effects of this medication.

To sum up, no drug· has been scientifically proved to help a male achieve an erection (except for the rare male with hormone deficiency). Most are only a waste of money, and some are potentially dangerous.

What Not to Do

The progress of rivers to the sea is not as rapid as that of man to error.

—Voltaire

Having discussed positive steps to remedy the problem of impotence, it is important to emphasize certain things that should *not* be done.

One should not assume that one's situation is hopeless, particularly considering the abundance of very successful treatment programs patterned after that introduced by Masters and Johnson. Even in those cases in which physical factors are responsible for impotence, so that the problem is not amenable to this type of treatment, there is still hope because of the availability of an implantable penile prosthesis.

One should not take the various medications that are sold over the counter and touted as effective. As I have noted, most are of no value whatsoever, and some are potentially dangerous.

One should not insert any object into the opening of the penis in order to stiffen it. Most such objects become lodged and must be removed surgically. An object frequently inserted inside the penis is a swizzle stick used to mix cocktail drinks. This object may be commonly chosen because it is convenient, particularly if a man has had several drinks and has a great desire for sex but finds his performance is inadequate.

Also, one should not put any type of ring around the

161

penis to make it stiff. Swelling generally occurs, and the ring cannot be removed. In many instances, surgery is necessary to relieve the predicament. One young male placed a solid metal ring at the base of his penis; several hours later, he found it could not be removed. It was like a ring stuck on a finger. He was seen in the emergency room where all the known tricks, including using soap and water and Vaseline, were attempted. The patient was taken to the operating room and anesthetized, but further attempts at removal were unsuccessful. The ring was made of cast iron, and no instrument available in the operating room could even scratch its surface. A consultation was then held with a plumber who happened to be on late duty at the hospital. After changing from his usual clothes into a surgical scrub suit, the plumber was invited into the operating room. After examining the patient, he said, "You'll have to cut it off." When asked what instrument could be used to cut off the ring, he responded, "Nothing will cut that ring; you'll have to cut off the penis." However, the penis was preserved by cutting off all its outer skin, which permitted the ring to slide off. The skin was then grafted back into place.

In an attempt to prolong an erection, some men or their female partners have applied a rubber band or tied a string to the base of the penis, the idea being to block the drainage of blood from the penis and thus keep it erect. However, this is extremely dangerous and may result in gangrene of the organ.

Some men who have difficulty achieving erections feel that they would perform more satisfactorily if their female partner were more sexually aggressive. Some men actually fantasize being attacked, or virtually raped, by their female partner. Many men would find that if they openly discussed this desire with their partners, the latter would willingly cooperate. However, most males are too embarrassed to bring up the subject. A man may then decide that if he withholds sex from his female partner, she will become ravenous for sex and thus fulfill all of his wishes. This ploy seldom works. The male finds himself becoming increasingly frustrated sexually as his desire for intercourse increases, and all the while, he is still uncertain as to whether he will be able to achieve an erection when the times comes. Meanwhile, his partner may not seem to notice that a significant amount of time has elapsed since the last sexual act, and this becomes of great concern to the male, who now wonders if she really ever wants to have sexual relations again. On the other hand, the female may be very aware of the sudden cessation of sexual activity, and she may erroneously conclude that her partner is no longer interested in sex. Thus, both parties draw the wrong conclusions and neither is benefited.

Some men who are having difficulty getting an erection wonder whether they might be successful if they were stimulated by pornographic material. Today, there is an abundance of such matter available either in the form of "adult movies" or very explicit magazines. There is no doubt that different men are stimulated by different types of subject matter. Thus, one finds movies or books dealing not only with heterosexual activity but also with lesbianism, group orgies, anal intercourse, and the so-called discipline films, in which women are subjected to various types of sadistic treatment.

Many impotent men have purchased either movies or magazines and have viewed them at home while attempting to masturbate or even while trying to engage in intercourse. Some have even devised rather elaborate setups that permit the movie to be shown on the ceiling above their bed. There is no doubt that males who are not having difficulties with erections may be readily stimulated by this material and will quickly develop a hard penis. But most men who are impotent do not find that this alleviates their problem. Despite the fact that they may find this material sexually arousing, they still can't get an erection.

Pornographic magazines advertise a dazzling array of medicines and devices that are supposed to solve such problems as erectile failure and premature ejaculation. Others are designed for the male who is unable to bring his female partner to orgasm. Creams and lotions are advertised that supposedly allow a male to "get it up again and again and again." "Hard-on" pills, as well as recipes that combine such aphrodisiacs as sarsaparilla and kola nut, are touted as promoting sexual potency on command. The various devices available boggle the mind. "Cock rings" are stated to provide a rock-hard erection. Rubber devices that fit around the penis are battery-powered and promise to produce vibrations that permit an erection. A vibrating plug that is inserted into the male's rectum is supposed to provide a sensation that causes an immediate erection.

For men who are having difficulty with a live partner, there are life-sized dolls with various-sized vaginas. These dolls can be placed in several positions. Some even are battery-powered and have a vibrating device built into the vagina or rectum. One of the more intriguing models even talks and moans in simulated ecstasy. Stores sell innumerable gadgets that could help an impotent man stimulate his partner. Vibrators, clitoral stimulators, and dildoes come in various sizes and shapes.

None of the above items has been scientifically proved to solve the problem of impotence, but it would be mind-boggling to calculate the millions of dollars spent on such devices by frustrated, desperate men who know of no other way to find help.

Acupuncture

Some impotent males have resorted to acupuncture as a hopeful remedy for erectile failure. Acupuncture is an ancient Chinese technique involving the manipulation of needles just beneath the skin in order to relieve pain or treat various illnesses. It originated in China some two thousand years ago and is now practiced in other parts of the world. Claims have been made for its effectiveness in treating or curing a variety of illnesses including insomnia, high blood pressure, and digestive diseases. In this country it has been used to treat painful joints and common maladies such as "tennis elbow." More recently, it has been used during surgery in place of conventional anesthesia.

Utilizing this technique, needles are inserted into specific points of the body depending on where the pain or illness is present. Elaborate charts exist pinpointing just where these needles should be placed. For impotence, it has been recommended that the needles be inserted at two main points: Kuan-Yuan, which is in the lower portion of the abdomen, and San-Yuan-Chiao, which is located in the lower leg near the ankle. Following insertion, the needles are rotated, usually by hand—though now electrical devices are available which will turn the needles.[8] The fact that acupuncture works in certain illnesses for some individuals is undeniable. At this time, an exact scientific explanation is lacking. Why some individuals benefit dramatically and others gain no relief from their pain or illness is unknown.

Acupuncture has no place at the present time in the treatment of impotence. While some individuals may have profited by taking treatments for erectile failure, most have not. Controlled scientific studies are not available showing the effectiveness of acupuncture for impotence. The desperate male should not waste his time or money trying this technique.

CHAPTER XII
THE FEMALE PARTNER

The Female Suffers, Too

No man is an island. . . .
                    —John Donne

While impotence may be catastrophic to the male, the difficulties that the female partner encounters should not be underestimated. A very solid relationship may be threatened or destroyed. The woman who does not understand her partner's "ups and downs" becomes confused and uncertain, and may experience frustration, guilt, and anger.

What heretofore has been a psychologically and physically satisfying experience no longer occurs. The warmth of the emotional relationship is diminished. The physical pleasure of intercourse and orgasm is missed. If the sexual frustration becomes intense, a woman may resort to masturbation, which for some is psychologically threatening. The embers of guilt feelings may be kindled.

B. J. M., a forty-one-year-old female, had always enjoyed a satisfactory sexual relationship with her husband. They had intercourse one to two times a week, and, more often than not, she enjoyed an orgasm. She began to notice that her husband's penis was not as firm as usual during their relations. Eventually he was unable to penetrate, and all attempts at intercourse ceased.

While she and her husband both recognized that a serious problem existed, there was no open discussion between them. B. J. M. began to feel "caged up" and realized that she greatly missed the psychic and physical satisfaction of intercourse. Finally, one morning when she was alone, she masturbated for the first time in more than seven years. Eventually, she was masturbating one to three times a week. This experience caused her great guilt feelings, for she felt that she was not being satisfied in a normal way.

The female may develop a sense of inadequacy, feeling that her partner's failure is her fault. She will review her own technique of lovemaking and try to find out where she has failed. She may then redouble her efforts during foreplay, but all to no avail. She may then develop doubts about her own physical attractiveness. Has her body begun to lose its appeal?

J. F., a thirty-seven-year-old female, knew her partner was impotent. They had not had successful intercourse for more than two months, which represented a significant departure from the usual one to two times a week. Taking the offensive one evening, she attempted to stimulate her male partner in virtually every imaginable fashion, and while he seemed to enjoy it, he still could not get an erection. J. F. tried to reconstruct her role during their most recent sexual activities to determine if her technique was unsatisfactory. Not being able to detect any deficiency, she began to feel that her own body had become less attractive to her partner. Gazing in the mirror, she began to notice many changes in her figure that had not been so apparent before. In fact, she was severely exaggerating any real changes that had occurred.

Finally, guilt feelings may turn into anger. The female knows she deserves to be satisfied and her partner is not providing her with that pleasure. Is he trying to punish her? Is he telling her that she is no longer important in his life? It doesn't take long for many women to wonder whether their partner is now having a sexual relationship with another woman.

D. G., a forty-four-year-old female, could not pinpoint when her husband's sexual interests began to wane. She had long since given up trying to arouse him sexually. She responded to her husband in a hostile fashion and felt strongly that he was purposely avoiding her sexually. She had long been suspicious that he was having an extramarital affair, and his lack of interest in her seemed to confirm this impression. In fact, her male partner was impotent from undiagnosed diabetes. This was discovered before their marriage dissolved, and they were able to save their relationship.

Since impotence takes its toll on both the male and female, the woman should be included in all counseling sessions. Her feelings must be appreciated by her impotent partner, and her questions must be satisfactorily answered by the physician or sex counselor.

What Do Women Really Want from a Sexual Experience?

There are three things I have always loved and never understood—painting, music, and women.

—Bernard de Fontenelle

Man's idea of what a sexual encounter should provide is seemingly very straightforward. If men are questioned as to their expectations of what should occur during sex, their answers are nearly all the same: erection, followed by penetration, which results in ejaculation and orgasm. During men's early sexual experiences, the female is often viewed as a challenge. It is not uncommon for one young friend to ask another, "How did you make out with Sue?" or "Did you get any?" Every female represents a new conquest. Many men have regarded introducing a virgin to sexual intercourse as attaining a special prize.

In short, a young man's attitude has been rather animalistic. It deemphasizes the emotional aspects of the male-female relationship. Some men never come to view sex as anything more than a simple pleasure for themselves.

It is difficult for many women to believe that this is all that a sexual encounter means to a male, and it hurts many who find that they are dealing with such a man. In such an instance, a woman feels that she is simply being used as an object of physical gratification. Unfortunately, many men do regard women in this fashion. Many men will have sex with a woman they consider unattractive, as long as she is willing.

As a man develops a more meaningful close relationship that may result in marriage, emotional feelings usually develop along with the purely physical ones. Sexual activity has a new meaning and seems to be less self-centered. If the relationship deteriorates, intercourse may become more mechanical and the man's goal once again becomes simply orgasm and ejaculation, although the challenge is now gone.

Most men really don't know what a woman desires from a sexual encounter. Some believe that all a woman expects is to be penetrated and serve as a repository of their semen. Other men don't really care what a woman wants as long as they are able to satisfy themselves.

If men better understood what women want from sex, they would be able to satisfy their partners in a much more meaningful way. Men would learn that an erection isn't all that is expected, and many who are impotent would find that they can well satisfy their partner, even without an erection.

The *Hite Report* has shed some light on the female's view of sexuality. This book reveals that women are fed up with the notion that sex involves only erection, penetration, ejaculation, and orgasm. When asked what changes they would like to see in their sex lives, women replied that they would like their male partner to be more sensitive toward their needs. They want more emotional expression and closer verbal communication. Women would like to see more tenderness and greater passion bestowed on them. Instead of having men dive for their genitals women would enjoy more kissing and caressing of other parts of their bodies.

Many women feel that men regard foreplay as the price they have to pay for eventual penetration, and that if they could get away with it, they would omit foreplay altogether.

Women are tired of the notion that they have to participate in intercourse just to satisfy their male partner. This goes beyond the simple feeling that they, too, deserve to have an orgasm. Some women would be just as happy with prolonged foreplay or with simple clitoral stimulation, and would prefer to dispense with penetration altogether. Many women want the right to decline sexual advances if they are not in the mood. They don't want simply to be "on call" to satisfy a man's needs.

When one is familiar with this view of sex, a lesbian relationship becomes more understandable. The female-female relationship is often more emotional than the female-male, and bodily contact can easily be prolonged.

If a male truly understands what a woman desires from a sexual encounter, he may be a potent lover even though he cannot have an erection. He may, in fact, be able to satisfy more women than the man who can always "get it up." If the male concentrates on the emotional aspects of his relationship with a woman, he will find that she is very receptive. This does not mean that physical activity is to be omitted; it is simply to be re-channeled. Hugging, caressing, kissing, and squeezing assume a more important role. Thus, a male who has been having difficulty achieving an erection should not avoid a sexual encounter. He may prove to be an excellent lover. And if this proves to be the case, his anxiety level may, with time, gradually be reduced to a point at which he will probably be able to achieve an erection. Even if he cannot because his impotence has a physical cause, he still may be a great lover and have the admiration of his female partner.

While a simultaneous orgasm between male and female may be ideal, it is not often reached. However, there is nothing wrong with one partner's climaxing before the other. Still, many men are uncertain about what to do if they ejaculate and have an orgasm before their female partner reaches climax. No hard-and-fast rules can be made, but if one excludes from consideration those males who have a persistent problem with uncontrollable ejaculation, and those females who just don't seem ever to reach orgasm, certain facts should be considered.

First, males should remember that since many women take longer to become sexually aroused than men, it may help to increase the length of foreplay. A male should also know that he may be able to stimulate his partner to orgasm by manual means if he has already ejaculated. Since female orgasms generally result from clitoral stimulation, this can be accomplished without actual penetration of the vagina by the penis. Men may also recall that not all women deem an orgasm essential during every act of intercourse. Many females derive significant physical and psychological satisfaction simply from engaging in the act of intercourse with their loved partner. Women's feelings toward this problem vary widely, and only an open discussion between the couple will really define what the female expects if her partner climaxes first. Some women will demand nothing of their male partner if he climaxes first, and others will insist on continued stimulation until they climax. Still others may choose to masturbate themselves to orgasm.

What the Female Can Do to Help the Impotent Male

It is better to avert a malady with care than to use physic after it has appeared.

—Shao Tze

Every female must understand that when a male cannot achieve an erection and have successful intercourse, it is a catastrophe for him. Because he has performed inadequately, the male's ego is shattered. He may feel anxious that his relationship is in jeopardy. He may feel guilty that he has not satisfied his partner. As one male said after experiencing several episodes of impotence, "If I can't be right, Doctor, then I would just as well be dead."

There is no question that the greatest contribution that a female can make is to be understanding. She must understand her partner's feelings and concerns. It is helpful if she reassures him that she is acquainted with this problem, at least through reading she has done, and that she knows there is help available. She must openly discuss with him anything she can do to reduce his anxiety or to stimulate him. A remark as simple as "Let's try again later" can be very supportive. On the other hand, a female partner's negative reaction or a casual statement such as "Don't start something you can't finish" or "Here we go again" may be devastating to the male.

The female must determine whether there is anything in her behavior or sexual performance that is contributing to the difficulty. If her partner signifies an interest or willingness to seek professional help, she must encourage him. If the counseling requires her presence, she should be a willing participant.

A female can salvage an impotent male's ego by encouraging him to satisfy her in other ways, such as by oral or manual stimulation. If she can have an orgasm utilizing these methods, the male will not feel that he has totally failed. And if she cannot have an orgasm, it is most reassuring if she acknowledges the fact that her total satisfaction does not depend on having an orgasm every time, and that she does enjoy those activities of which the male is capable.

Studies have shown that the frequency of sexual intercourse is extremely important to the male. Most men would like to have intercourse at least three to four times a week, and many would be happy with five to seven times each week. If there is a marked difference in the partners' sexual desires, both will be unhappy. As I stated previously, a reasonable compromise must be achieved. The first step is an open discussion of each person's feelings on the matter.

Those women who sense that their partners are simply bored with their sexual relationship should try a new approach. Few women will seriously condone a relationship with another woman, but they may introduce a change in their pattern of sexual activity by utilizing different forms of stimulation, such as oral sex, or by trying new positions.

The most common position for sexual intercourse in the United States is the so-called missionary position, in which the female lies on her back and the male is on top, facing her. In this position the male can easily control the rate of thrusting. Some men who are having difficulty achieving a good erection report that they can insert the partially erect penis more easily in this position. However, the male-superior position has several disadvantages, which include rapid ejaculation by many men because of vigorous thrusting and maximum penile stimulation.

Most American couples will sometimes use the female-superior position. This permits the female more control over the rate and depth of penile penetration of the vagina, and allows the woman to take a more active role during intercourse. This position is often recommended by sex therapists for women who are having difficulty achieving orgasm.

The third most commonly used position in this country

is probably side-to-side. Many men report that they can control ejaculation best in this position.

The rear-entry position has several variations. Both partners may be lying on their sides, or the woman may be bending over or perhaps leaning on her elbows and knees. Some couples do not approve of this position, since there is no face-to-face contact, which they feel denotes a lack of intimacy. Also, many women complain that this permits little clitoral stimulation. However, this can be achieved manually if necessary.

There are numerous other coital positions, including penetration while both partners are sitting or standing. Couples should realize that no one position is either "normal" or "abnormal." However, whatever positions are used should be acceptable to both partners.

Some couples have reported success with a vibrator. These are readily available in many department stores, adult book stores, and by mail order. Do they work? Sometimes increased tactile stimulation of the genitalia beyond that provided by manual stimulation is helpful. A vibrator applied to the perineum, between the bottom of the scrotum and the anus, sometimes facilitates an erection, particularly if the penis is masturbated simultaneously. However, most often the benefit is only transitory and disappears as the novelty wears off.

An older couple should increase the length of foreplay. Any particularly pleasing maneuver should be repeated. In other words, whatever is stimulating should be utilized to its greatest advantage. With age, simple touching, caressing, and holding one another increases in importance. Older men may not ejaculate, and a woman should not force the issue, for her partner may still derive great pleasure from intercourse.

Any female whose male partner is having difficulty with his sexual functioning should assess her own understanding of the specific problem and should also evaluate their relationship. The questions below, if thoughtfully answered, will provide insight that may assist in resolving the male's sexual inadequacy.

Self-evaluation for the Female

1. Have you and your partner openly discussed this problem?
2. Are you aware of any factor that may be causing his difficulty?
3. Do you know which sexual activities are most stimulating and pleasing to your partner?
4. Does your partner try to stimulate you in a way that you really enjoy?
5. What percentage of the time do you have an orgasm or find yourself sexually satisfied?
6. Do you have sexual relations more or less often than you would like?
7. Do you have sexual relations more or less often than your partner would like?
8. Do you believe your partner is having an affair with another woman?
9. Does your relationship with your partner seem to be a solid one, even though there may be a problem with his sexual functioning?
10. If your partner attempts intercourse and is unable to penetrate because the penis is not firm enough, what do you do? Do you make any remarks? If so, are the remarks meant to encourage him, or do you belittle his inadequate performance?
11. If your partner cannot achieve an erection sufficient to penetrate, are there other techniques he can utilize that would be sexually satisfying to you? If so, have you discussed these with him?
12. Have there been any changes in your personal appearance or hygiene that might lessen your partner's interest in you?
13. Has your partner discussed the possibility of seeking help for his sexual problem?
14. Have you encouraged your partner to seek assistance?
15. Would you be willing to accompany your partner to see a physician or sexual counselor?

CHAPTER XIII
WHAT'S NEW?

The man with a new idea is a crank until the idea succeeds.

—Mark Twain

Three new tests have been devised that help to differentiate whether a man's failure to achieve an erection is due to psychological difficulties (psychogenic impotence) or a physical abnormality (organic impotence). These tests are the nocturnal tumescence device, the radioisotope penogram, and thermography.

The nocturnal penile tumescence device fits around the penis like a collar. It notes an increase in the circumference of the penis when it swells. Sleep research, which has burgeoned over the last decade, reveals that there are regularly recurring periods of sleep associated with a characteristic brain wave pattern and with a rapid movement of the eyes in either a vertical or a horizontal direction. These are called rapid eye movements (REM). Periods of sleep in which REMs occur are also associated with dreaming. It is at these times that erections occur. REM sleep occurs approximately four to five times a night and is associated with a strong erection, which lasts approximately fifteen to twenty-five minutes each time. When one nurse was told of this, she commented, "What a waste!"

Erections during REM sleep occur from birth to old age. However, the length of time that erections last decline as age increases. During adolescence, 90 percent of REM sleep is associated with a good, strong erection, whereas between the ages of forty and fifty, this time declines to approximately two-thirds that of young adults.

Dreams associated with anxiety during REM sleep result in the rapid loss of an erection, just as an anxious person usually cannot get an erection while he is awake. The importance of being able to detect erections during REM sleep is that in cases of psychological impotence, the erections are generally normal in terms of their duration and degree. Thus, the physician learns whether his patient has a physical or a psychological problem. Impotence resulting from physical causes is characterized by an absence of erections during REM sleep.

Nocturnal penile tumescence devices were formerly utilized only in laboratory settings, but now, thanks to progressive engineering techniques, they may be used at home and are certain to become more widespread in the future. Impotent men will be asked to wear the device at home during the night, and a recording will be made on a graph, which a doctor can later analyze to determine whether an erection has occurred.

Another useful test that is being used to differentiate psychological from physical impotence is the radioisotope penogram. This test has received much attention in Japan. Since an erection cannot occur without a strong flow of blood to the penis, this test measures that flow. Following the intravenous administration of a radioisotope (99M technetium), blood flow is determined. Sexual stimulation is then accomplished by showing pornographic material, and blood flow is again calculated. Those males showing no increase in blood flow to the penis are suspected of having a physical disease, while those having good erections and an increased blood flow are considered to have psychological problems.

Another diagnostic test being utilized to determine the cause of impotence is thermography. This test measures a rise in the skin temperature of the penis when an erection occurs. An erection is caused by increased blood flow, which in turn causes an increase in the temperature of the skin. This test is currently being used at the

Yamaguchi University Medical School in Ube, Japan. The men being tested assume a comfortable, prone position. A special thermographic camera is then placed above the penis. The men are stimulated sexually in two ways. First, they are given a substance that contains yohimbine and strychnine, two potentially dangerous drugs, both of which help to promote an erection. Then the men are shown a very explicit sex film that is extremely stimulating psychologically. When an erection occurs, it is easily measured by an accompanying rise in skin temperature.

It is believed that men who show a rise in penile skin temperature yet claim they cannot achieve an erection during intercourse are impotent for psychological reasons. However, for those impotent men who show no increase in skin temperature, physical illness may be the root of their problem.

Blood pressure measurement may also be used to assess potency. The measurement of penile blood pressure is taken with a special blood-pressure cuff in order to assess potency. It has been demonstrated that normal pressure in the penis is very close to the normal blood pressure in the arm as detected by conventional measurement. Another means of determining blood flow to the penis is to use a Doppler flowmeter. This technique utilizes ultrasound, which is translated into audible signals representing the velocity of blood flow. These tests are not yet widely used, and it is not yet certain that they will be broadly employed by physicians.

Another, older test that is used to help assess the impotent male is the Minnesota Multiphasic Personality Inventory (MMPI). This is a 566-item true-false test that allows comparison of a given patient's responses with those of patients known to be normal and abnormal. This permits the preparation of a personality profile and helps to point out those patients who may be impotent because of an emotional conflict or depression.

At this time, nocturnal penile tumescence testing is probably the most reliable and objective method available for determining whether impotence is psychological.

There are two new forms of treatment for impotence

that may be beneficial: bromocriptine and biofeedback. Bromocriptine is a drug currently in use in Europe. Claims have been made for its effectiveness in improving fertility and sexual performance in both males and females. However, there is conflicting information available. In Italy, seven impotent men treated with the medication reported an improvement, but in England investigators noted no benefit for fifteen impotent males. Before any conclusions can be drawn, more men who are sexually dysfunctional must be tested. This medication is not yet approved for the treatment of impotence in the United States.

Biofeedback is receiving a great deal of attention in this country. In using this technique, one monitors one's physical response to stimuli and tries to achieve control over one's bodily activities. This method is being applied to the treatment of impotence. A kit is available that contains an amplifying device that permits a male to hear these sounds arising from penile pulsations that occur as he gets an erection. Stimulation is provided by a female voice on an audio cassette. Speaking in a very suggestive manner and using erotic phrases, the female instructs the male to relax so that he may achieve an erection. The male can monitor his penile response and try to control the erection process.

Further studies are needed to scientifically evaluate the effectiveness of both bromocriptine and biofeedback.

CHAPTER XIV
SELF-EVALUATION FOR THE MALE

"Know thyself" is indeed a weighty admonition. But in this, as in science, the difficulties are discovered only by those who set their hands to it. We must push against a door to find out whether it is bolted or not.

—Montaigne

Any male who is impotent will profit from his own honest analysis of his personal situation, and a female will gain insight into her partner's difficulty through this analysis. The following questions, if they are carefully considered, will allow a male or female to put the problem in perspective. The information that is collected will be very valuable to any physician or counselor who seeks to aid the male having sexual difficulties. It is much easier to answer these questions in an honest and realistic fashion if one does so in the quiet, unpressured setting of the home rather than in the doctor's office, where one may feel rushed.

The importance of these questions will be appreciated by those who have read the preceding chapters. An interpretation of the answers is included.

Part One: General Information
  1. What is your specific complaint?
     a. Inability to get an erection.
     b. Ejaculation prior to insertion of the penis into the vagina.

   c. Lack of ejaculation.

   d. Loss of interest in sex.

   e. Penis does not stay firm enough.

   f. Failure to have an orgasm.

2. Have you ever had an erection?

3. When was the last time you had what you would consider a complete, normal erection followed by ejaculation?

4. When you first became impotent, what significant events were occurring in your life? Were you having any financial, health, or marital difficulties?

5. Are you currently happy with your spouse or partner?

6. Do you believe she is having an affair with another man?

7. Do you feel it is important that your female partner climax during every episode of intercourse?

8. Do you have strong sexual desires?

9. Is your female partner less interested in sex than you are?

10. Have you and your female partner ever discussed each other's attitudes toward sex with each other? Do you know the following about your partner?

   a. Does she enjoy oral sex?

   b. How often during intercourse does she have an orgasm?

   c. Does she climax with simple thrusting, or would she prefer masturbation either during or after intercourse?

   d. Does she believe you are having intercourse or attempting to have coitus too often or too infrequently?

e. Is there any particular time of the month when she seems to have heightened sexual interest?

f. Does she prefer one coital position more than another?

The answers to the foregoing questions will elucidate your specific problem. They will help you to discover when your problem began and how long it has been going on. Insight will also be gained into your general attitude toward sexual intercourse.

Interpretation

1. *What is your specific complaint?*

   Your answer to this question should define clearly your real complaint.

2. *Have you ever had an erection?*

   If you have never had an erection in your life, you are suffering from primary impotence. This suggests either a serious physical problem or a deep-seated emotional one that will require professional counseling.

3. *When was the last time you had what you would consider a complete, normal erection followed by ejaculation?*

   It is important to try to date the onset of your difficulty. Impotence of short duration is usually more easily treated than impotence that has been present for a long time.

4. *When you first became impotent, what significant events were occurring in your life? Were you*

having any financial, health, or marital difficulties?

Very often, it may be possible to pinpoint a specific cause of impotence. Anxiety or depression generated by specific difficulties may become apparent. Recognizing the relationship between a specific problem and the onset of impotence is the first step toward improvement.

5. *Are you currently happy with your spouse or partner?*

If your emotional relationship with your spouse or partner is not solid, it is not surprising that sexual difficulties are present. Impotence may simply be a reflection of the fact that the entire relationship is failing.

6. *Do you believe she is having an affair with another man?*

If your partner has found it necessary to have sexual intercourse with another male because of your sexual problem, your relationship is on very shaky ground and you probably will need professional counseling.

7. *Do you feel it is important that your female partner climax during every episode of intercourse?*

If you feel that you must ensure that your female partner has an orgasm during every sexual encounter, you may be placing unrealistic demands upon yourself. This in turn may cause your sexual failure.

8. *Do you have strong sexual desires?*
If you have a strong sex drive but are impotent,

you will probably be highly motivated to solve your problem. Absence of sex drive suggests a poor prognosis for cure.

9. *Is your female partner less interested in sex than you are?*

Sometimes a male becomes impotent because he feels that his partner is not genuinely interested in sexual intercourse. Your answer here will help you to decide whether your partner has a sincere interest in sex and in seeing that your problem is resolved.

10. *Have you and your female partner ever discussed each other's attitudes toward sex with each other?*

Most males have not openly discussed with their female partner her attitude toward, and response to, sex. A sound relationship includes exchanging thoughts and feelings about sexual activity.

Part Two: Physical Causes of Impotence

1. What medicines are you taking?

2. Are you a diabetic?

3. What surgical procedures have you had?

4. Have you ever had priapism?

5. How much alcohol do you drink on an average day?

6. Do you use heroin, cocaine, or marijuana?

7. Do your legs ache when you walk more than two blocks?

8. Have you sustained any back injuries or a fractured pelvis?

9. Do you have multiple sclerosis?

Interpretation

1. *What medicines are you taking?*

   Many commonly used medications may cause failure of erection, inability to ejaculate, or a decreased sex drive.

2. *Are you a diabetic?*

   Fifty percent of diabetics will become impotent.

3. *What surgical procedures have you had?*

   Many common surgical procedures may cause sexual difficulties.

4. *Have you ever had priapism?*

   A prolonged erection may prevent future erections.

5. *How much alcohol do you drink on an average day?*

   Alcohol is considered by many to be the most common physical cause of the inability to get an erection.

6. *Do you use heroin, cocaine, or marijuana?*

   Many of the illegal drugs thought to enhance sexual functioning actually inhibit performance.

7. *Do your legs ache when you walk more than two blocks?*

Poor blood supply to the pelvis and legs, usually caused by atherosclerosis, may cause impotence.

8. *Have you sustained any back injuries or a fractured pelvis?*

Serious injuries to the nervous system may prevent erections.

9. *Do you have multiple sclerosis?*

Multiple sclerosis can affect many parts of the body, including the penis.

Answers to the preceding questions are discussed in Chapter VII. They will help you to decide whether you are suffering from any bodily ailments that may prevent you from having an erection. Some of these physical causes may be readily treated—for example, by discontinuing a medicine that is causing impotence. On the other hand, many are treatable only with a penile prosthesis.

Part Three: Psychological Causes of Impotence

1. Are you able to get a good, firm erection at some times but not at others?

2. Does erectile difficulty occur only with a certain partner?

3. Can you masturbate and ejaculate with a firm penis?

4. Do you awaken at night or in the morning with an erection?

5. Have you recently been depressed about anything?

6. Have you ever had a homosexual experience?

7. Do you find the female anatomy disgusting or repulsive?

8. Have you had a heart attack, or are you fearful of dying during intercourse?

9. Are you currently unusually anxious about anything?

10. Are you usually afraid of not being able to accomplish intercourse successfully?

11. Does your wife or sexual partner belittle you or make remarks if you cannot get an erection?

12. Are you having difficulty getting your wife pregnant?

13. Do you have cancer?

Interpretation

1. *Are you able to get a good, firm erection at some times but not at others?*

   If you get an erection at any time that is sufficient to complete the act of intercourse, yet at other times you are impotent, it is quite likely that your difficulty is psychological. This is also the case if you can have intercourse at certain times but not at others.

2. *Does erectile difficulty occur only with a certain partner?*

   If you are impotent only with a certain partner, but can perform successfully with someone else,

187

there is not likely to be any physical problem causing impotence.

3. *Can you masturbate and ejaculate with a firm penis?*

If you can masturbate with a normally hard penis, the cause of your impotence *must* be psychological.

4. *Do you awaken at night or in the morning with an erection?*

If so, your impotence must be caused by psychological difficulties. In fact, if you answered yes to any of the above questions, there is probably a strong psychological factor involved in your problem.

5. *Have you recently been depressed about anything?*

Depression can adversely affect many parts of the body, including the penis.

6. *Have you ever had a homosexual experience?*

A homosexual experience resulting in fear, anxiety, or guilt can prevent a male from getting an erection when attempting intercourse with a female.

7. *Do you find the female anatomy disgusting or repulsive?*

Some men are simply turned off by the female genitals.

8. *Have you had a heart attack, or are you fearful of dying during intercourse?*

Anxiety following a heart attack may keep males from resuming a normal sexual life.

9. *Are you currently unusually anxious about anything?*

An anxious male usually cannot achieve an erection.

10. *Are you usually afraid of not being able to accomplish intercourse successfully?*

The fear of sexual failure may create a vicious cycle that prevents successful performance.

11. *Does your wife or sexual partner belittle you or make remarks if you cannot get an erection?*

An unsympathetic female partner may inhibit the male from having an erection.

12. *Are you having difficulty getting your wife pregnant?*

Pressure to achieve a pregnancy may cause difficulty with erections.

13. *Do you have cancer?*

A male with cancer may become sufficiently depressed to find himself unable to perform sexually.

The psychological causes of impotence are discussed at length in Chapter VI.

Part Four: Attitude toward Treatment of Impotence

1. *How important is it to you to be able to achieve an erection and have intercourse?*

2. *Would you be willing to consult a physician or sex counselor to help you with your problem?*

3. *Would your wife or sexual partner be willing to consult a physician or sex therapist with you?*

Your answers to these questions should indicate how much the problem of impotence bothers you. They will also signify whether or not you are genuinely willing to seek help and whether you can count on your partner to stand by you.

As already noted, these questions and your answers are intended only as a framework to help you to understand your problem and to aid a professional sex counselor or physician in managing your case. Many men who have answered these questions will figure out for themselves whether the cause of their impotence is psychological or physical. Most men are relieved once they have made their own diagnosis. If you have pinpointed your difficulty, rereading the appropriate section in this book will help you to fully appreciate your problem. In addition, it will permit you to understand the form of treatment that may help you.

> *It is clearly necessary to provide good, honest, realistic education—for the lay public as well as for physicians and medical students—about human sexuality if the fears and anxiety associated with the experience or anticipation of impotence are to be relieved. Regardless of the cause, impotence is terrifying to the man who lacks understanding of sexuality and sexual behavior.*
>
> —*Disease-a-Month*, May 1975

NOTES

CHAPTER I: Why This Book Was Written

1. "Current Thinking on Sources of Sexual Conflict in Marriage," *Medical Aspects of Human Sexuality* 12 (August 1978): 110.
2. Wilhelm Stekel, *Impotence in the Male* (New York: Liveright Publishing Corp., 1927).
3. John A. Blazer, "Married Virgins—A Study of Unconsummated Marriages," *Journal of Marriage and the Family* 26 (May 1964): 213.
4. A. B. Chernick and B. A. Chernick, "The Role of Ignorance in Sexual Dysfunction," *Medical Aspects of Human Sexuality* 4 (February 1970): 114.

CHAPTER III: A Look at the Past

1. William F. Gee, "A History of Surgical Treatment of Impotence," *Urology* 5 (March 1975): 401.
2. John F. O'Connor, "Effectiveness of Psychological Treatment of Human Sexual Dysfunction," *Clinical Obstetrics and Gynecology* 19 (June 1976): 449.
3. Alan J. Cooper, "Factors in Male Sexual Inadequacy: A Review," *Journal of Nervous and Mental Disease* 4 (October 1969): 337.

CHAPTER IV: Understanding Erections

1. William H. Masters and Virginia E. Johnson, *Human Sexual Response* (Boston: Little, Brown & Co. 1966).
2. Ellen B. Vance and Nathaniel N. Wagner, "Written Descriptions of Orgasm: A Study of Sex Differences," *Archives of Sexual Behavior* 5 (January 1976): 87.

3. Wilhelm Stekel, *Impotence in the Male* (New York: Liveright Publishing Corp., 1927).

CHAPTER V: How Often Does the Average Man Have Intercourse?

1. C. E. Pearlman and L. I. Kobashi, "Frequency of Intercourse in Men," *Journal of Urology* 107 (February 1972): 298.
2. Morton Hunt, "Sexual Behavior in the 1970's," *Playboy* 20 (October 1973): 84.
3. A. C. Kinsey, W. B. Pomeroy, and C. R. Martin, *Sexual Behavior in the Human Male* (Philadelphia: W. B. Saunders Co., 1948).
4. Richard von Krafft-Ebing, *Psychopathia Sexualis* (New York: G. P. Putnam's Sons, 1969).

CHAPTER VI: Psychological Causes of Impotence

1. H. K. Malhotra and N. N. Wig, "Dhat Syndrome: A Culture-Bound Sex Neurosis of the Orient," *Archives of Sexual Behavior* 4 (September 1975): 519.
2. Kenneth Walker and Eric B. Strauss, *Sexual Disorders in the Male* (Baltimore: The William and Wilkins Co., 1948).
3. Alan J. Cooper, "Factors in Male Sexual Inadequacy: A Review," *Journal of Nervous and Mental Diseases* 149 (October 1969): 337.
4. Alfred Auerback, "Sex vs. the Late, Late Show," *Medical Aspects of Human Sexuality* 4 (January 1970): 33.
5. W. Lederer, *The Fear of Women* (New York: Grune and Stratton, 1968): 281.
6. Norman B. Levy, "Sexual Adjustment to Maintenance Hemodialysis and Renal Transplantation: National Survey by Questionnaire: Preliminary Report," *Transactions of the American Society for Artificial Internal Organs* 19 (1973): 138.
7. Art Buchwald, "Never on Monday, Either," *Medical Aspects of Human Sexuality* 7 (January 1973): 100.

CHAPTER VII: Physical Causes of Impotence

1. Robert Mendex, W. F. Kiely, and J. W. Morrow, "Self-Emasculation," *Journal of Urology* 107 (June 1972): 981.

2. S. C. Evins, Tom Whittle, and S. N. Rous, "Self-Emasculation," *Journal of Urology* 118 (November 1977): 775.

3. Lewis C. Mills, "Drug-Induced Impotence," *American Family Physician* 12 (August 1975): 104.

4. Arthur Lipman, "Drugs Associated with Impotence," *Modern Medicine* 45 (May 1977): 81.

5. A. E. Comarr, "Sexual Concepts in Traumatic Cord and Cauda Equina Lesions," *Journal of Urology* 106 (September 1971): 375.

6. John Money, "Phantom Orgasms in Paraplegics," *Medical Aspects of Human Sexuality* 4 (January 1970): 90.

7. Theodore M. Cole, "Sexuality and Physical Disabilities," *Archives of Sexual Behavior* 3 (July 1975): 389.

CHAPTER VIII: Other Sexual Crises

1. Paul Dormont, "Sexual Clock Watchers," *Medical Aspects of Human Sexuality* 8 (November 1974): 87.

2. Otto F. Ehrentheil, "A Case of Premature Ejaculation in Greek Mythology," *Journal of Sex Research* 10 (May 1974): 128-131.

3. Stephen B. Levine, "Inability to Ejaculate Intra-Vaginally," *Medical Aspects of Human Sexuality* 12 (July 1978): 27.

CHAPTER IX: Myths and Fallacies

1. Andrew W. Green, "Fundamentals of Clinical Cardiology: Sexual Activity and the Postmyocardial Infarction Patient," *American Heart Journal* 89 (February 1975): 246.

2. Gerhart S. Schwarz, "Devices to Prevent Masturbation," *Medical Aspects of Human Sexuality* 7 (May 1973): 141.

3. M. Freund and J. E. Davis, "A Follow-Up Study of the Effects of Vasectomy on Sexual Behavior," *Journal of Sex Research* 9 (August 1973): 241.

4. James L. Nash, and John D. Rich, "The Sexual After-effects of Vasectomy," *Fertility and Sterility* 23 (October 1972): 715.

5. C. E. Charny, R. Suarez, and N. Sadoughi, "Castration in the Male," *Medical Aspects of Human Sexuality* 4 (May 1970): 80.

6. Pierre Berton, *The Dionne Years: A Thirties Melodrama* (New York: W. W. Norton & Co., Inc., 1977), 69.

7. P. M. Yap, "Koro—A Culture-bound Depersonalization Syndrome," *British Journal of Psychiatry* 3 (1965): 43.

8. S. W. Bondurant, and S. C. Cappannari, "Penis Captivus: Fact or Fancy?," *Medical Aspects of Human Sexuality* 5 (March 1971): 224.

CHAPTER X: Sexual Performance and Aging

1. P. H. Gebhard, "Factors in Marital Orgasm," *Journal of Social Issues* 22 (April 1966): 88.

2. Eric Pfeiffer, Adriaan Verwoerdt, and Glenn C. Davis, "Sexual Behavior in Middle Life," *American Journal of Psychiatry* 128 (April 1972): 82.

3. James Leslie McCary, "Sexual Advantages of Middle-Aged Men," *Medical Aspects of Human Sexuality* 7 (December 1973): 139.

4. Carl K. Pearlman, and L. I. Kobashi, "Frequency of Intercourse in Men," *Journal of Urology* 107 (February 1972): 298.

5. Eric Pfeiffer, "Geriatric Sex Behavior," *Medical Aspects of Human Sexuality* 3 (July 1969): 19.

6. Robert L. Solnick, and James E. Birren, "Age and Male Erectile Responsiveness," *Archives of Sexual Behavior* 6 (January 1977): 1.

CHAPTER XI: Treatment for the Impotent Male

1. Ira B. Pauly and Steven G. Goldstein, "Physicians'

Ability to Treat Sexual Problems," *Medical Aspects of Human Sexuality* 4 (October 1970): 24.

2. W. O. Ward, "The Hypnotherapeutic Treatment of Impotence," *Virginia Medical Journal* 104 (June 1977): 389.

3. William F. Gee, "A History of Surgical Treatment of Impotence," *Urology* 5 (March 1975): 401.

4. Robert D. Lutz, "External Penile Prostheses," *Medical Aspects of Human Sexuality* 10 (March 1976): 123.

5. Mary Simpson and Thomas Schill, "Patrons of Massage Parlors: Some Facts and Figures," *Archives of Sexual Behavior* 6 (November 1977): 521.

6. Leo E. Hollister, "Drugs and Sexual Behavior in Men," *Life Sciences,* Pergamon Press, 17 (September 1975): 661.

7. George Lang and Arthur M. Sackler, "The Lovelore of Lust-Provoking Foods," *Sexual Medicine Today* 2 (December 1978): 17.

8. Leong T. Tan, Margaret Y-C Tan, and Ilza Veith, *Acupuncture Therapy: Current Chinese Practice* (Philadelphia: Temple University Press, 1973).

BIBLIOGRAPHY

Cooper, Alan J. "Treatments of Male Potency Disorders: The Present Status." *Psychosomatics* 12 (July–August 1971): 235.

Fisher, Charles, et al. "The Assessment of Nocturnal REM Erection in the Differential Diagnosis of Sexual Impotence." *Journal of Sex and Marital Therapy* 1 (Winter 1975): 277.

Gay, George R., and Sheppard, Charles W. "Sex in the Drug Culture." *Medical Aspects of Human Sexuality* 6 (October 1972): 28.

Geboes, K.; Steeno, O.; and DeMoor, P. "Sexual Impotence in Men." *Andrologia* 7 (1975): 217.

Karacan, Ismet, et al. "Sleep-Related Penile Tumescence as a Function of Age." *American Journal of Psychiatry* 132 (September 1975): 932.

Kinsey, Alfred C.; Pomeroy, W. B.; and Martin, C. E. *Sexual Behavior in the Human Male.* Philadelphia: W. B. Saunders Co., 1948.

Levine, Stephen B. "Marital Sexual Dysfunction: Ejaculation Disturbances." *Annals of Internal Medicine* 84 (May 1976): 575.

Levine, Stephen B. "Marital Sexual Dysfunction: Erectile Dysfunction." *Annals of Internal Medicine* 85 (September 1976): 342.

Masters, W. H., and Johnson, V. E. *Human Sexual Inadequacy.* Boston: Little, Brown and Co., 1970.

Masters, W. H., and Johnson, V. E. *Human Sexual Response*. Boston: Little, Brown and Co., 1966.

Pfeiffer, Eric, and Davis, Glenn C. "Determinants of Sexual Behavior in Middle and Old Age." *Journal of the American Geriatrics Society* 20 (April 1972): 151.

Reckless, J., and Geiger, N. "Impotence as a Practical Problem." *Disease-a-Month* (May 1975): 1–40.

Schellhammer, Paul, and Donnelly, John. "A Mode of Treatment for Incarceration of the Penis." *Journal of Trauma* 13 (February 1973): 171.

Schiavi, Raul C., and White, Daniel. "Androgens and Male Sexual Function: A Review of Human Studies." *Journal of Sex and Marital Therapy* 2 (Fall 1976): 214.

Semans, J. H. "Premature Ejaculation: A New Approach." *Southern Medical Journal* 49 (April 1956): 353.

Shirai, M., and Nakamura, M. "Diagnostic Discrimination between Organic and Functional Impotence by Radioisotope Penogram with 99mTc04." *Tohoku Journal of Experimental Medicine* 116 (May 1975): 9.

Stearns, E. L., et al. "Declining Testicular Function with Age." *American Journal of Medicine* 57 (November 1974): 761.

Weiss, Howard D. "The Physiology of Human Penile Erection." *Annals of Internal Medicine* 76 (May 1972): 793.

INDEX

Index

THE INDISPENSABLE CONSUMER'S GUIDE TO DRUGS

The People's Pharmacy

JOE GRAEDON

★ Tells which drugs when taken in combination with common foods like milk or coffee can be dangerous—even fatal!

★ Shows how to treat common ailments with home remedies

★ Lists drugs harmful to pregnancies

★ Reveals common drugs that affect sexual desires and performance

★ Tells how to save money with generic substitutes for expensive prescription drugs

★ Evaluates over 200 brand name products, including aspirin, antacids, tranquilizers, sleeping pills, birth control methods, vitamins, antibiotics, drugs affecting the heart, and much more!

"BELONGS SOMEWHERE NEAR EVERY HOUSEHOLD MEDICINE CHEST."
New York Magazine

Avon 43216 $4.95
PHAR 11-78